Knitting with Knifty Knitter®

Babies & Toddlers .20

Cuddle up 40

Let's play. 58

Family crafts 74

Index . . . .

W9-BFD-966

Introduction

The goal of Knifty Knitter® products is to make the old art of knitting more accessible to modern generations. The looms are so easy to use that it's tempting to think there are limits to what the Knifty Knitter looms can do. However, designer Shannon Erling has proved that assumption wrong.

Shannon is a knitting beginner turned expert, all thanks to vision, innovation, and the Knifty Knitter collection. In this book Shannon shares projects that she designed and created using the Knifty Knitter Long Looms, the Knifty Knitter Flower Loom, and the Knifty Knitter Pom-Pom & Tassel Maker. Shannon shows that with the Knifty Knitter line, there are hundreds of creative possibilities! There is no wrong way to knit with the Knifty Knitter looms. The stitches and techniques explained in this book are simply Shannon's suggestions.

There are projects for every taste and skill level, from darling shrugs to clever toys. In *LoomCrafts™ with Knifty Knitter®*, every project shows that knitters of all types can produce amazing results on the Knifty Knitter looms.

Shannon Erling

Note from the Designer

I must admit I never considered myself a knitter. I had tried other needlecrafts, but knitting never appealed to me. It was difficult to get good results and too time consuming for a mother of four with a busy schedule. That all changed when I was introduced to Knifty Knitter products. Knitting became something I could do and have fun doing. I was amazed that my children would actually fight over who got the projects when I finished. For me the best result is that something I made by hand means more than something purchased in a store. Here's hoping my projects will help your ideas flow and you will have fun creating something that will bring joy to your family and friends.

Create a
Slip Knot

The slip knot is one side of a bow when you tie your shoes. I prefer using a slip knot on the first peg used instead of using a single hitch because it holds the yarn in place for you.

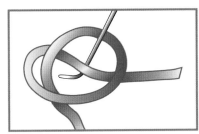

1. Hold yarn in left hand about 8" from end. With right hand make circle with yarn. Hold circle together between index finger and thumb to prevent it from slipping away.

2. With working yarn behind circle, catch it from front and pull through circle to form loop.

3. Place new loop onto first peg and gently pull on both starting tail and working yarn to tighten loop snuggly to first peg.

or

Secure to the
Anchor Peg

You can use a single hitch on the anchor peg to begin knitting instead of using a slip knot on the first peg.

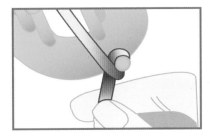

1. Use thumb and first finger to make loop in yarn.

2. Place loop on anchor peg.

3. Pull loop tight.

Note: Loop usually holds in place securely and is easy to remove to continue wrapping yarn. If the loop slips, use two single hitches.

Keeping it Loose
Wrapping

A common problem for beginners is wrapping the yarn so tightly on the pegs that it's difficult to knit off, or lift the bottom loop over the top loop(s). When you lift a yarn loop up and over the peg, the yarn pulls the yarn that travels between the pegs, not just the yarn looped around the peg. To wrap loosely, there are several things you can do:

1. Make sure there is plenty of slack between skein of yarn and loom. Pull yarn from skein and keep small pile of yarn in lap or to side. Pulling yarn from skein at same time as wrapping loom puts tension on yarn and pulls stitches tight.

2. You can also thread yarn through Knifty Knitter® Weave Tool and hold tool to wrap yarn (figure 1). This will help maintain even tension when wrapping pegs.

3. When wrapping loom, hold yarn on last peg with one hand while wrapping next peg with other hand.

4. When picking up loop to knit off, pull it towards your body, but not too much, and then lift it up and over. Push remaining loop down to bottom of peg to lengthen distance between that loop and next loop to be wrapped.

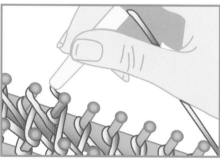

figure 1

Knitting Off
Variations

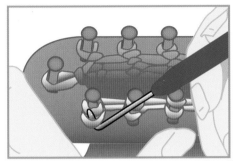

figure 2

one-over-one stitch

Wrap loom twice and knit off, taking the bottom loop over top loop and peg (figure 2).

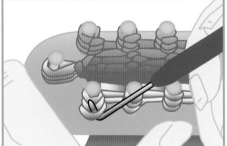

figure 3

one-over-two stitch

Wrap loom three times and knit off, taking bottom loop over the top two loops and peg (figure 3).

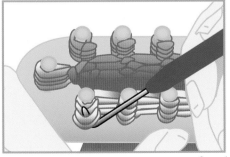

figure 4

two-over-two stitch

Wrap loom four times and knit off, taking bottom two loops over top two loops (figure 4).

Tube Knitting

Tube knitting is knitting around the loom in a continuous circle creating a tube of fabric.

1. Secure yarn with slip knot to first peg or with single hitch knot to anchor peg.

2. Pull yarn to inside of loom between first two pegs to be wrapped (figure 5).

3. E-wrap loom by wrapping yarn around far side of each peg, going completely around peg, and crossing inside of loom (figure 6). Keep yarn loose. Continue wrapping until all pegs are wrapped.

4. Slide yarn on each peg toward bottom of peg.

5. Continue wrapping around pegs until you have two rows of loops (figure 7) or number required by pattern.

6. Keep loose yarn in place on anchor peg with single hitch or just hold in place until you knit it in place.

7. Using hook, knit off. Repeat steps 2 through 7 until you reach desired length.

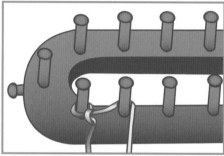

figure 5

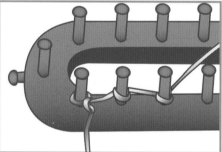

figure 6

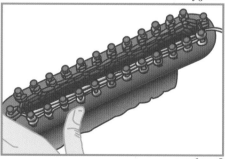

figure 7

Panel Knitting

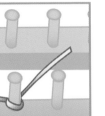

figure 8

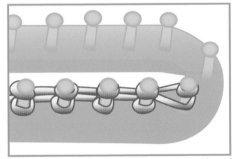

figure 9

Panel knitting creates a single sheet of fabric instead of a tube of fabric. You work back and forth on the loom instead of in rounds.

1. E-wrap yarn around pegs (figure 8) until you have one loop on each peg (or until desired width is reached).

2. Turn at last peg. Wrap last peg one more time (figure 9).

3. Continue wrapping back to first peg.

4. Knit off and continue wrapping and knitting off back and forth until knitting is desired length.

Making an
I-Cord

1. Knit using only two pegs. Place slip knot onto one peg (not anchor peg). Wrap peg next to first peg twice (figure 10). Then wrap first peg again (figure 11).

2. Knit off. Continue wrapping in figure-eight design and knitting off until I-cord is desired length, gently pulling I-cord behind pegs to straighten and tighten.

3. To end cording, take first peg loop over second peg loop and knit off. Cut yarn, push through remaining loop, and pull tight to knot.

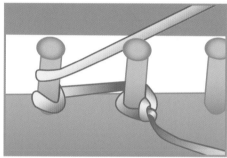

figure 10

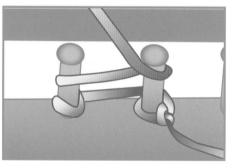

figure 11

Ribbed Stitch

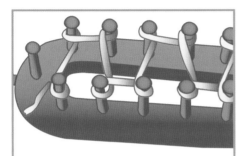

figure 12

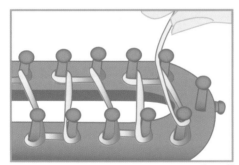

figure 13

To create a ribbed stitch, you will use both sides of the loom (both the bottom and the top pegs). DO NOT USE THE TWO END PEGS WHEN USING THIS STITCH.

1. Tie slip knot on first bottom peg or wrap first bottom peg clockwise.

2. Wrap peg just above it and top peg next to it counterclockwise.

3. Wrap peg just below and bottom peg next to it clockwise(figure 12). Repeat steps 1 & 2 until reach you end of loom.

4. Maintain pattern of two pegs counterclockwise on top and two pegs clockwise on bottom until you reach end of loom. Wrap last peg twice before returning (figure 13). *continued on page 8*

Ribbed *Stitch* *continued*

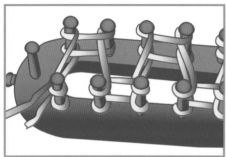

figure 14

5. Wrap with same pattern going back to beginning peg (figure 14). From now on wrap loom once and knit off, and then wrap back and knit off. Continue this way until knitting reaches desired length.

Note: Some patterns require you use two strands of yarn for thickness. Treat as one strand and knit off, pulling bottom loops over top loops.

Alternated or Interrupted **Ribbed Stitch**

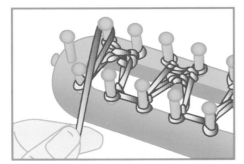

figure 15

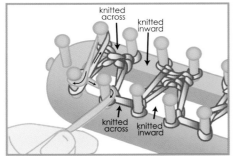

knitted across

knitted inward

knitted across

knitted inward

figure 16

The alternated or interrupted ribbed stitch is very similar to the ribbed stitch, except you will interrupt rows of knitting by switching direction for just one row or up to 5 rows, then switching back to the original direction. This creates the appearance of rings.

1. After knitting desired number of ribbed stitch rows in one direction, switch direction as wrapping loom. Still wrap loom in pairs of two, wrapping top pegs counterclockwise and bottom pegs clockwise. However, start going down instead of up first (figure 15), so you knit across where you once knitted inward (figure 16).
    continued on page 10

Alternated or Interrupted
Ribbed Stitch *continued*

2. Wrap first top peg counterclockwise and then wrap first bottom peg and bottom peg next to it clockwise. Continue pattern until end of row of wrapping pegs on top counterclockwise and bottom counterclockwise, going across where you once went inward (figure 17).

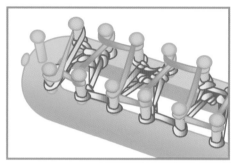

figure 17

3. Knit one row or up to five rows (depending on pattern directions) this way and then switch back to original ribbed stitch direction for desired number of rows.

Adding Width

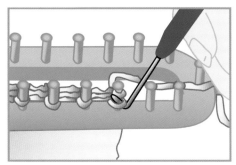

figure 18

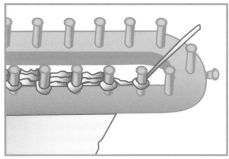

figure 19

Increasing your knitting is adding width by increasing the number of stitches to enlarge an area to accommodate shaping, such as when creating arms for sweaters.

1. Start in middle of loom, leaving space on sides to increase width. Knit as usual until you reach end of row you want to increase (figure 18). Wrap an empty peg (figure 19).

2. Continue wrapping as usual, but do not knit new peg until you have as many loops added to it as your regular knitted section. For example, if you have three loops on each peg, do not knit until next wrapping when you have three loops on new peg.

Sometimes you need to increase more than one new peg. If so, just wrap as many new pegs as required by pattern. Do not knit whole new section until required loops have been added.

Tapering *Off*

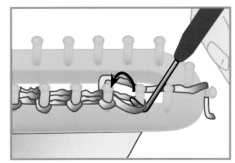

figure 20

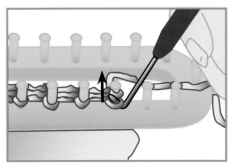

figure 21

Decreasing your knitting is tapering off by reducing the number of stitches to taper an area to accommodate shaping, such as when creating arms for sweaters.

1. On row to be decreased, take end loop that will be decreased (figure 20) and add it to peg next to it.

2. Knit off (figure 21) and then continue with knitting project.

Sometimes you need to decrease more than one peg or loop. If so, continue steps 1 & 2 until you have decreased the number of pegs required.

Changing *Colors*

How to Start a New Color or Make a Stripe

1. Cut first color of yarn leaving 4" end. Attach new color to peg on edge of loom, leaving 3" end.

2. Wrap new color around first peg, and then continue around (figure 22).

3. Knit off and continue wrapping. After knitting two or three rows, tie ends together with square knot to prevent gaps. Weave in loose ends when project is finished.

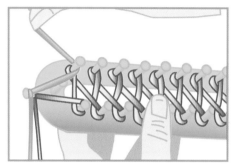

figure 22

Making a *Square Knot*

The square knot holds tightly in place and will not slip.

1. Hold 2 strands of yarn, one strand in each hand.

2. Pass strand A (left) over and under strand B (right).

3. Cross strand B (now left) over and under strand A (now right).

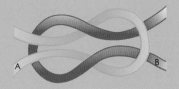

4. Tighten.

Joining **Yarn**

If you run out of yarn before an item is complete, you must attach more yarn mid-project. To join yarn, use one of the following methods:

1. Use square knot to tie old and new yarn together and continue knitting (figure 23). Use fabric glue or super glue if knot slips on slippery yarn. However, knot can create bump in project. Knots can also pop out later and be visible. Weave ends in when project is finished.

2. Stop knitting with old yarn (figure 24) and start knitting with new yarn (figure 25) at the end of the loom. (May require pulling out previously knitted stitches). Leave 6" of old and new yarn hanging. Knit two or three rows and then knot two threads at the end so knot is on the end of weaving. Weave ends in when project is finished.

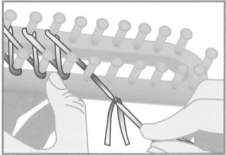

figure 23

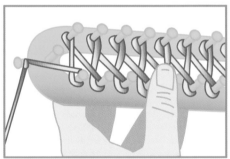

figure 24

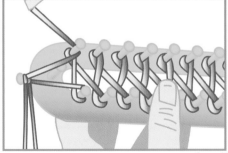

figure 25

Follow instructions given for each project until piece is finished. Remove work from loom using one of following finishes.

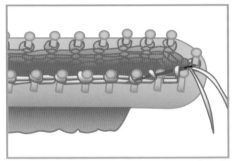

figure 26

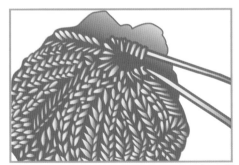

figure 27

The gather finish is a method of finishing that is used to close tubes of knitting.

1. Cut yarn leaving 12" end. Thread end through yarn needle. Starting with first peg, slip needle through loop on peg and pull loop off peg (figure 26).

2. Repeat for all pegs around. Pull yarn tight (figure 27), knot, and weave end into project.

Mattress *Finish*

The mattress finish creates a loose edge instead of the tighter edge made with the other finishes. This stitch secures each loop in place without pulling the loops. It can be used for panel, double, ribbed, and interrupted ribbed stitches.

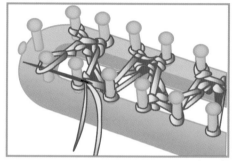

figure 28

1. Cut yarn leaving enough to sew through edge of project. Thread needle and sew through last loop knitted (figure 28).

2. Instead of removing loop from peg, go back around and sew through same loop again (figure 29). Then remove loop from loom. Go to next loop and sew through this loop twice as well and remove from loom.

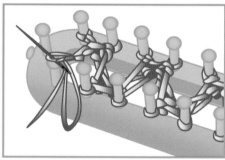

figure 29

3. Repeat steps 1 & 2 until all loops are removed. Knot.

Making a
Mattress Seam

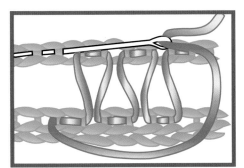

figure 30

The mattress seam is a method of sewing together knitted pieces. It is neat and nearly invisible.

1. Layer pieces to be attached side by side with front side facing you.

2. On one piece, pull edge stitch slightly away from stitch next to it to reveal horizontal bar. Pull yarn needle and yarn under and through bar. You do not need to pull stitch tight yet.

3. Insert needle under parallel horizontal bar on second knitting piece, and pull yarn through. Work back and forth between two pieces, pulling through one piece and then other piece until you have three or four loose rows.

4. Gently and firmly pull needle and yarn in direction of seam (not towards you) to tighten yarn and seal up gap between two pieces. Do not pull so much that seam puckers.

5. Continue stitching between two pieces until gap is entirely sealed and pieces are completely attached. Finish by connecting two corner stitches at ends and weaving yarn end through backside of pieces.

Hidden *Seams*

This stitch creates hidden seams when sewing two open-looped edges of knitting together that are still on the loom, such as on shoulders.

1. Before removing from loom, use yarn needle to thread contrasting color of yarn through each panel to prevent loops from pulling out (figure 31). This yarn will be removed later once project is sewn. Gently remove knitting from loom.

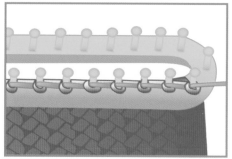

figure 31

2. Place right sides of knitting together and using crochet hook take one loop from front panel and loop it through same loop on back panel (figure 32). Take back loop through front loop. Push back one loop now on crochet hook, move to next two loops, and loop back through front loop. Then loop second peg set through first peg's loop. Repeat to end of knitting.

3. Knot or sew down remaining loop on crochet hook. Remove contrasting yarn.

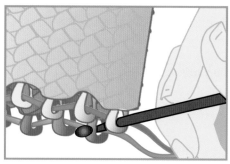

figure 32

Glossary of Terms

Anchor peg: The peg(s) on the outside of the loom, which can be used to secure your yarn before and after you wrap the loom.

E-wrap: A basic wrap of the yarn around the pegs. It crosses on the inside of the loom, and looks like a cursive lowercase e when viewed from above.

End/corner peg: The pegs on the top side of the loom at each end. These enable you to tube knit on the long loom.

Ending tail: The last segment of yarn remaining after you finish knitting.

Knit off: Bringing a yarn loop up over one or more loops on the same peg, taking that loop off the peg, and placing it in the inside of the loom.

Starting tail: This is the very beginning string of your yarn; the part that hangs off the loom near where the slip knot sits on the first peg.

Working yarn: The yarn that you are currently using to wrap the loom.

Yarn Weight

  SUPER FINE 1 FINE 2 LIGHT 3

   MEDIUM 4 BULKY 5 SUPER BULKY 6

If you want to make thinner yarn work for a bulkier project, just use more than one strand of yarn as one. You can also use more loops on the peg to make it bulkier. You can knit the one-over-two stitch or even the two-over-two stitch (see page 3).

Looms Used

Blue Long Loom: 22" long with 62 pegs

Green Long Loom: 18" long with 52 pegs

Yellow Long Loom: 14" with 38 pegs

Pink: 10" with 26 pegs

Pom-Pom & Tassel Maker

Flower Loom: 3½" diameter with 12 pegs

Babies & Toddlers

Take some time to make something sweet for your little one! Snuggle your baby in the soft blankets, darling sweater, and adorable toys in this section designed by Shannon to greet your new arrival. Personalize your projects and make beautiful homemade heirlooms with ease on the Knifty Knitter® looms.

Baby Hooded
Chick Blanket

Making the Blanket

1. Knit with yellow yarn around entire blue loom using panel knitting and one-over-one stitch. Remember you will not be knitting around entire loom to create a tube—instead, knit back and forth around loom to create a large square blanket. Depending on yarn used, width of blanket can be anywhere from 24" to 28". Stop knitting when width of your blanket is same as length.

2. To remove blanket from loom, cut yarn so you have enough to sew blanket off loom. Thread yarn needle and sew through each loop twice before removing loop from loom.

Making the Hood

1. Use 16 pegs on one side of loom using panel knitting and one-over-one stitch. When you have 4" of knitting, fold this over and knit so you have 2" band for hood.

continued on page 24

Techniques
Panel knitting (see page 5)
One-over-one stitch (see page 3)
Decreasing (see page 12)
I-cord (see page 6)
Mattress seam (see page 17)

Materials Needed
Knifty Knitter® Long Loom—Blue
7 skeins yellow bulky yarn
2 black or dark brown buttons or felt circles (for eyes)
2" square orange fabric or felt sewed together (for beak)
Sewing thread (to attach eyes and beak)
Yarn needle

BULKY 5

I used:
7 skeins Bernat® Baby Lash, Bulky (1¾ oz/50g), #67615 Soft 'n Sunny

Tip: If you decide to use standard size yarn or baby yarn for this blanket, you will need to use two yarn threads at one time and treat them as one thread as you use one-over-one stitch. Do not expect to use as many skeins of yarn as above.

Finished Size
Blanket: about 25" square
Hood: 10" x 6"

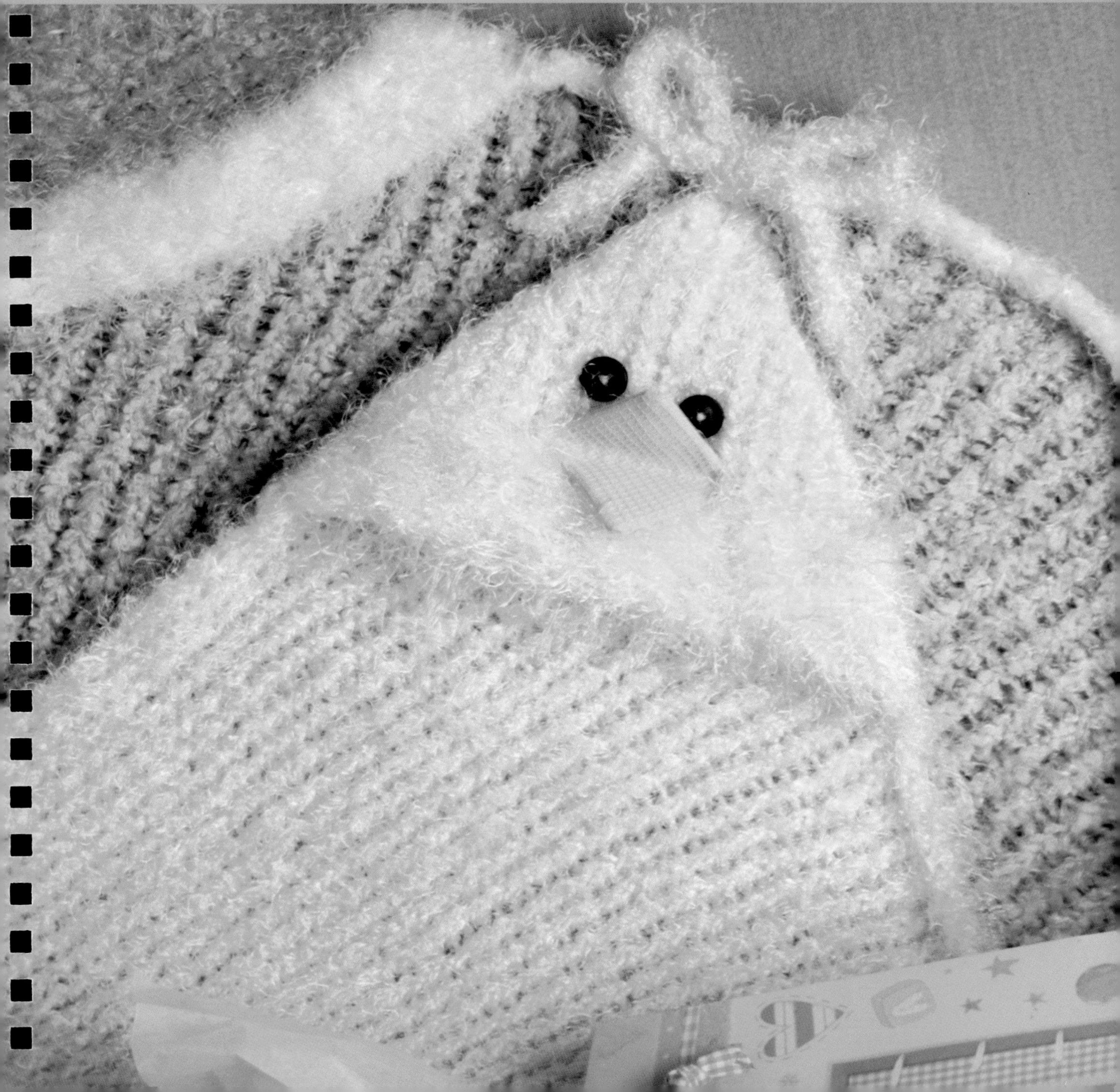

Baby Hooded
Chick Blanket *continued*

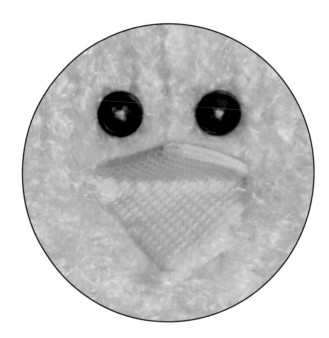

2. Knit four rows, and decrease two ends until you are using only 14 pegs instead of 16.

3. Knit two more rows then decrease two ends until you are only using 12 pegs. Knit two rows and decrease ends again to 10 pegs. Repeat this pattern of knitting two rows and decreasing two ends until you are down to last two pegs.

4. Take working yarn through last loop, and pull and knot to finish it off. Hood will be about 10" wide and 6" tall.

5. To attach hood, lay hood right side up on any corner of square blanket. Make sure fuzzy side of blanket is outside. Sew hood onto blanket using yarn needle with mattress seam.

Decorating the Face of the Chick

1. Find center of hood and sew 2" square orange fabric or felt in center just above band on hood. To form triangle beak, turn 2" square on angle and sew from corner to corner.

2. Sew on eyes just above corners of beak.

Creating the Bow for the Hood

1. Use yellow yarn to make I-cord about 18" long.

2. Tie I-cord into bow and sew with thread to top of hood.

Baby Hooded
Winter Blanket

Techniques
Panel knitting (see page 5)
One-over-one stitch (see page 3)
Decreasing (see page 12)
I-cord (see page 6)
Mattress seam (see page 17)

Materials Needed
Knifty Knitter® Long Loom—Blue
Knifty Knitter Pom-Pom & Tassel
Maker
7 skeins blue super bulky yarn
1 skein white super bulky yarn

 SUPER BULKY 6   Yarn needle

I used:
7 skeins Patons® Allure, Super Bulky
(1¾ oz/50g), #04128 Aquamarine
1 skein Patons® Allure, Super Bulky
(1¾ oz/50g), #04005 Diamond

Finished Size
Blanket: about 25" square
Hood: 10" x 6"

Any creative color combinations can be used, including red and white for a Santa look.

Making the Blanket

Use same instructions as Chick Blanket only use blue yarn.

Making the Hood

1. Use 16 pegs on one side of loom and panel knit using one-over-one stitch with white yarn. When you have 4" of knitting, fold this over and knit so you have 2" white band for hood.

2. Change to blue yarn and knit four rows, and then decrease two ends until you are using only 14 pegs instead of 16.

3. Knit two more rows then decrease two ends until you are only using 12 pegs. Knit two rows and decrease ends again to 10 pegs. Repeat this pattern of knitting two rows and decreasing two ends until you are down to last two pegs.

continued on page 26

Baby Hooded
Winter Blanket continued

4. Take working yarn through last loop, and pull and knot to finish it off. Hood will be about 10" wide and 6" tall.

5. To attach hood, lay hood right side up on any corner of square blanket. Make sure fuzzy side of blanket is outside. Sew hood onto blanket using blue yarn and yarn needle with mattress seam.

Creating the White Cording

1. Use white yarn to create I-cord. Measure around blanket. Knit I-cord to length. Sew cording onto blanket edge using mattress seam. Or sew as you go while knitting I-cord to make sure you have enough cording to go around whole blanket.

2. Attach cording with mattress seam just below white band on hood, and end when you reach white band on other side of hood.

Making a Pom-Pom for the Hood

1. Use white yarn on Pom-Pom & Tassel Maker to make pom-pom.

2. Thread loose yarn ends through top of hood and knot on inside of hood.

Baby's First *Quilt*

Instructions

1. Knit using panel stitch on 26 pegs and use both colors of yarn at same time. Both threads will act as one thicker piece of yarn as you knit with one-over-one stitch. Form a square that is 8 ½" x 8 ½". Remove square by sewing up through each loop twice with working yarn before removing from loom (this will prevent gathering). Create seven knitted squares.

2. Cut seven squares that are 8 ½" x 8 ½" from end of solid-colored fabric (purple). This will be used as backing for knitted squares (to prevent batting from coming through when you wash quilt).

3. Cut eight squares that are 8 ½" x 8 ½" from patterned fabric (colored pastel squares).

4. Lay out checkerboard pattern of five rows of three squares. Top row, center row, and bottom row will have one knitted square with material backing in center surrounded by two patterned

continued on page 30

Techniques
Panel knitting (see page 5)
Two-over-two stitch (see page 3)

Materials Needed
Knifty Knitter® Long Loom—
any loom with 26 small pegs
1 skein light baby yarn (pinkish purple)
1 skein darker baby yarn (purple)
Fiberfill or cotton stuffing
2½ yards solid color (purple) fabric,
½ yard of another solid color (pink fabric)
1 yard patterned fabric
(colored pastel blocks)
Sewing thread and sewing machine
or needle
Yarn needle (metal is needed for tying quilt)

LIGHT
3

I used:
1 skein Bernat® Softee Baby, Light
(5 oz/140g), #30185 Soft Lilac
1 skein Bernat® Baby Coordinates, Light
(6 oz/170g), #01010 Soft Mauve

Note: When using bulkier weight yarns you only need to use one strand of yarn and knit one-over-one, or one-over-two if you prefer a thicker consistency.

Finished Size
32" x 48"

Baby's First
Quilt continued

squares. Other two rows will have patterned square surrounded by two knitted squares with solid material backings. Make sure right sides of material are facing up. When you sew two squares together by hand or with sewing machine, make sure knitted square is sandwiched between material blocks. When you sew longer rows of sewn squares together, make sure to use pins to keep squares and corners straight.

5. Once all blocks are sewn together, cut two widthwise and two lengthwise strips 3" wide out of solid-colored fabric (pink) to form border. These strips are same length and width as sewn squares. Cut four squares that are 3½" x 3½" out of patterned fabric (colored pastel squares). These will be corner blocks.

6. Sew lengthwise strips onto sides of quilt with right sides together.

7. Then sew 3½" x 3½" block onto each end of widthwise long strip. Sew these strips to top of quilt.

8. Cut two widthwise and two lengthwise strips 3" wide out of other solid-colored fabric (purple) to form final border. This time make sure widthwise strips are at least 3" longer on each end (or you can add other corner blocks if you wish). Sew these onto quilt.

9. Cut backing for quilt out of solid-colored fabric (purple) that matches size of top of quilt. Sew backing and quilt together with right sides facing each other, but leave 12" opening in middle bottom of quilt to add stuffing and sew up later.

10. Cut stuffing to size of quilt. Roll stuffing lengthwise on each end and stuff in opening. Roll out each end of stuffing and spread stuffing out equally. Sew up opening on machine or by hand.

11. Use yarn and metal yarn needle to tie quilt. Sew and knot each corner of square and in middle of each square (make sure you cut threads evenly). It also helps to tie and knot in middle of 3½" corner blocks.

Baby Bear &
Baby Bear Blanket

Baby Bear
Techniques
One-over-one stitch (see page 3)
Panel knitting (see page 5)
Tube knitting (see page 4)
Mattress seam (see page 17)

Materials Needed
Knifty Knitter® Long Loom—Pink
Knifty Knitter Pom-Pom & Tassel Maker
1 skein light colored bulky yarn
1 skein darker colored bulky/furry yarn
Yarn needle
Fiberfill or cluster stuffing
Buttons, felt, or material circles (for eyes)
Rattle (for inside—optional)
Ribbon or small knitted scarf (for neck)

BULKY 5

I used:
1 skein Lion Brand® Homespun® Baby,
Bulky (3 oz/85g), #800-101 Pink Carnation
1 skein Patons® Be Mine, Bulky
(1¾ oz/50g), #63420 Furry Rose

Note: You could also use bulky white yarns and add a red scarf for a polar bear. The color choices are up to you, but use bulky and furry yarns.

Finished Size
9" tall

Instructions for Baby Bear

1. You will use two yarns at one time that will act as one thread as you knit with one-over-one stitch. You will be panel knitting on one corner of pink loom. Start in center of pink loom (6 pegs from edge of loom) and e-wrap yarn around corner of loom to center (6 pegs from edge of loom) on other side of loom. Wrap and knit back and forth until leg is 5" long. Knot and cut yarn, but do not remove leg panel from loom.

2. Begin knitting on other side of loom in same way (starting on sixth peg from other side), and create another 5" long leg panel. You will not be cutting yarn or removing either leg panel from loom. This way legs will be attached to body tube.

3. Begin winding around entire loom using tube knit. Create 11" long tube for bear's head and body. Head will be 5½" and body will be 5½" when completed.

4. Sew through each loop at top of tube with yarn needle, and gather all loops tightly together and knot. Turn bear inside out.

5. Create arms by panel knitting on 10 pegs and knitting back and forth until
continued on page 32

Baby Bear &
Baby Bear Blanket *continued*

you have 3½". Gather loops together and sew down side of arm. Turn inside out and stuff. Create two.

6. Stuff head of bear with softball-sized ball of stuffing, and baseball-sized ball of stuffing for snout. Add two golf-ball-sized bunches of stuffing to top of head for ears. Stuff body. Add rattle if desired.

7. Sew with yarn needle and gather bottom panel of one leg on bear, knot with square knot, and then sew up leg of bear. Stuff leg with stuffing, and then sew down other side of leg, stuff with stuffing, and gather at bottom.

8. Sew in and out around neck (5½" from top). Pull to desired look, knot, and add ribbon or scarf on top for decoration.

9. Sew arms on below neck on each side with mattress seam.

10. For ears, sew with yarn in and out between golf-ball-sized balls of stuffing and head. Sew circle around snout (baseball-sized ball of stuffing) and gently gather and knot when you have desired look.

11. Create pom-pom nose and pom-pom tail on Pom-Pom & Tassel Maker. Sew on nose to top of snout and tail

to back. Sew on eyes. If desired, sew arms and legs together to keep bear in sitting position.

Baby Bear Blanket Techniques
One-over-two stitch (see page 3)
One-over-one stitch (see page 3)
Panel knitting (see page 5)
Tube knitting (see page 4)
I-cord (see page 6)

Materials Needed
Knifty Knitter® Long Loom—Pink
(for bear head)
Knifty Knitter Long Loom—Green
(for blanket)
Knifty Knitter Pom-Pom & Tassel Maker
1 skein light colored bulky/furry yarn
3 skeins darker colored bulky/furry yarn
Fiberfill or cluster stuffing
Vinyl or leather material (for eyes)
Yarn needle

BULKY 5

I used:
1 skein Patons® Allure, Bulky
(1¾ oz/50g), #04005 Diamond
3 skeins Bernat® Baby Lash, Bulky
(1¾ oz/50g), #67420 Precious Pink

Finished Size
26" long x 20" wide

Baby Bear & *Baby Bear Blanket* *continued*

Baby Bear Blanket Instructions

Making the Head

1. Using one-over-two stitch, tube knit 5½" long tube on pink loom using light yarn.

2. Use yarn needle to gather loops together tightly and knot. Turn head inside out.

3. Stuff and sew head of bear following instructions for baby bear. Sew around bottom of head about two rows up with yarn needle, gather loosely and knot to form neck. If desired, tie ribbon around neck after you attach blanket.

4. Use darker yarn to create accents by sewing smiling mouth and adding color to ears. Use Pom-Pom & Tassel Maker to create nose.

5. For eyes, cut vinyl or leather in circle and then in half. Cut small triangle cuts to add highlights to eyes. Sew on with thread and needle.

Making the Blanket

1. Panel knit with one-over-one stitch around entire green loom with darker yarn. Knit back and forth around loom to create large square blanket about 20" wide and 20" long.

2. Sew through each loop twice with working yarn before you remove it from loom to prevent blanket from gathering together.

3. Tuck one side of blanket into bear head opening. Sew with yarn and needle in and out through neck (where you gently gathered it before) and blanket to secure in place.

Optional: Create an I-cord with lighter-colored yarn to sew on exposed edges of blanket. Sew I-cord using mattress seam onto blanket edge. Make sure you have enough cording to go around whole blanket.

Toddler Sweater

Techniques
One-over-two stitch (see page 3)
Panel knitting (see page 5)
Increasing (see page 11)
Mattress seam (see page 17)
Hidden seams (see page 18)
I-cord (see page 6)

Materials Needed
Knifty Knitter® Long Loom—Green
4 skeins multicolored medium yarn
12" long white separating zipper
Sewing thread and needle
Yarn needle

MEDIUM
4

I used:
4 skeins Bernat® Cottontots®, Medium
(3 oz/85g), #91713 Koolade

Note: If using bulkier weight yarns, use the one-over-one stitch.

Finished Size
Sizes 12–24 months

Instructions

Body of the Sweater

1. Use one-over-two stitch and panel knit, start on one side of loom (12 pegs from end) and knit around entire loom to peg next to starting peg (12 pegs from other end). This will create a zipper opening in center front, since you will not be removing sweater from loom as you create arm and neck openings later. Panel knit around entire loom for 20 rows (or 2½") and then fold bottom of knitting back on loom and knit to form a band.

2. Panel knit for 60 more rows (or 7½").

3. Create opening for arms by decreasing two end/corner pegs.

4. Now concentrate on one side of zipper opening. Use 12 pegs on one side and knit back and forth for 38 more rows (or 4¾").

5. Create neck opening by using Knifty Knitter hook and crochet six of the 12 loops over until you only have six loops at end of loom that will create the shoulder. You will knit last crochet loop into loop next to it to prevent loops from pulling back out. (You can also just sew twice through each of the six loops and knot securely instead of using hook).
continued on page 36

Toddler
Sweater continued

6. Remaining six pegs at end of loom will form shoulder by panel knitting for 10 more rows (or 1¼"). Knot and cut yarn, but leave on loom. Then duplicate steps 4–6 on other zipper side of 12 pegs.

7. Now panel knit on back 24 pegs of sweater for 38 rows (or 4¾").

8. To create shoulders for back of sweater, panel knit on six pegs at each end of 24 pegs for 10 rows (or 1¼"). You will ignore middle 12 pegs and knit with them later. Sew bright colored piece of yarn or thread through each front and back shoulder piece so you can remove them from loom. Only remove shoulder pieces from loom.

9. Create hood by increasing by 10 pegs on each side of the 12 you still have on loom. Panel knit for 80 rows (or 10") on the 32 pegs now e-wrapped on loom. Sew with brightly colored yarn or thread through loops on loom and gently remove loops from loom.

10. Using hidden seams you will now be sewing hood and shoulders together. Make sure you have right sides together as you sew front shoulder to back shoulder. Hood is folded in half (16 loops on one side and 16 loops on other side) and sewn with right sides together.

Creating the Sleeves

1. Use 18 pegs that are centered on one side of green loom. Center them so you have room to increase rows later to make sleeves wider at top.

2. Panel knit for 20 rows (or 2½"), then fold bottom back on loom to form band and knit for 10 more rows (or 1¼").

3. You will now be increasing by two pegs (one peg on each end of knitting) every 20 rows until you are using 24 pegs or one whole side of green loom (that means three times you will increase by two). When you are done your sleeves should be as long as your hood (80 rows long or 10").

4. Sew up each sleeve using mattress seam.

Decorative Touches

1. Hood trim is created by using 43 pegs and panel knitting 20 rows (or 2½"), and then folding bottom back on loom and knitting to form band. Take yarn needle and sew twice through each loop before removing from loom. Pin this add-on piece to hood so it goes evenly around hood, and then sew onto hood using mattress seam.

2. Create two I-cords that are 40" long. Thread one I-cord into hood and knot both ends of I-cord. Thread other I-cord into waistband and knot both ends of I-cord.

3. Pin zipper into place just above waistband and up to start of hood. Sew in place with thread or use sewing machine.

Toy Bag

Instructions

1. Using blue yarn, tube knit with one-over-two stitch around entire blue loom for 2½" or 20 rows.

2. Change yarn color to multicolored yarn and tube knit with one-over-one stitch around entire loom for 12½".

3. Change color back to blue yarn and knit one-over-two stitch for 10 rows or 1¼".

4. Create opening for handles to go through. Decrease two end/corner pegs and start panel knitting with one-over-two stitch on one side of loom for 20 rows or 2½". Knot and cut working yarn but do not remove loops from loom. Begin panel knitting on other side for 20 rows or 2½". Do not knot or cut working yarn this time.

5. Resume wrapping entire loom (which means you will be increasing end/corner pegs back on loom) and tube knitting with one-over-two stitch around entire loom for 10 rows or 1¼". Sew through each loop twice with yarn needle before you remove loops from loom.

6. Fold blue band to inside of bag and sew down band with mattress seam.

7. Create two I-cords with multicolored yarn that are each 36" long.

8. Thread one I-cord with both ends coming out one opening in blue band, and thread other I-cord with both ends coming out other opening in blue band. Knot ends of each I-cord securely together.

Techniques
Tube knitting (see page 4)
Panel knitting (see page 5)
One-over-two stitch (see page 3)
One-over-one stitch (see page 3)
I-cord (see page 6)
Mattress seam (see page 17)

Materials Needed
Knifty Knitter® Long Loom—Blue
1 skein medium yarn
1 skein multicolored medium yarn
Yarn needle

I used:
1 skein Bernat® Cottontots®, Medium (3 oz/85g), #90129 Blue Berry
1 skein Bernat® Cottontots®, Medium (3 oz/85g), #91713 Koolade

Note: If using bulkier weight yarns, use the one-over-one stitch.

Finished Size
12" x 20"

Cuddle up

Get cozy with these warm Knifty Knitter® projects! Cuddle up with soft and stylish shrugs, scarves, and hats for cool winter days, or curl up with clever blankets and pillows perfect for relaxing at home. Discover all the comfortable creations you can make on your Knifty Knitter looms!

Girl's Shrug

Instructions

1. Tube knit 10 rows around entire yellow loom with one-over-one stitch. Decrease knitting on end/corner pegs of loom until you are only using pegs across from one another.

2. Wrap loom using ribbed stitch; knit until you reach length required to go around your girl's shoulders.

3. When you have achieved desired length, sew through each loop with brightly colored thread or piece of yarn to prevent loops from pulling loose when you remove them from loom. Use yarn needle and mattress seam to sew together matching loops on bottom and top of knitting. One end is straight knitting and other end is ribbed stitch. Remove brightly colored thread or piece of yarn after you finish sewing project together in circle.

4. Add crystal or regular buttons to front piece for decoration. You could also create knitted piece 10 rows wide to place around front piece and sew together in back to form tube (this would help it gather tighter in front).

Techniques
Tube knitting (see page 4)
One-over-one stitch (see page 3)
Decreasing (see page 12)
Ribbed stitch (see page 7)
Mattress seam (see page 17)

Materials Needed
Knifty Knitter® Long Loom—Yellow
3 skeins bulky yarn
Crystal or regular buttons
Yarn needle

BULKY 5

I used:
3 skeins Lion Brand® Watercolors, Bulky
(1¾ oz/50g), #980-301 Pink Petals

Finished Size
I made 29" long shrug, but size it according to child.

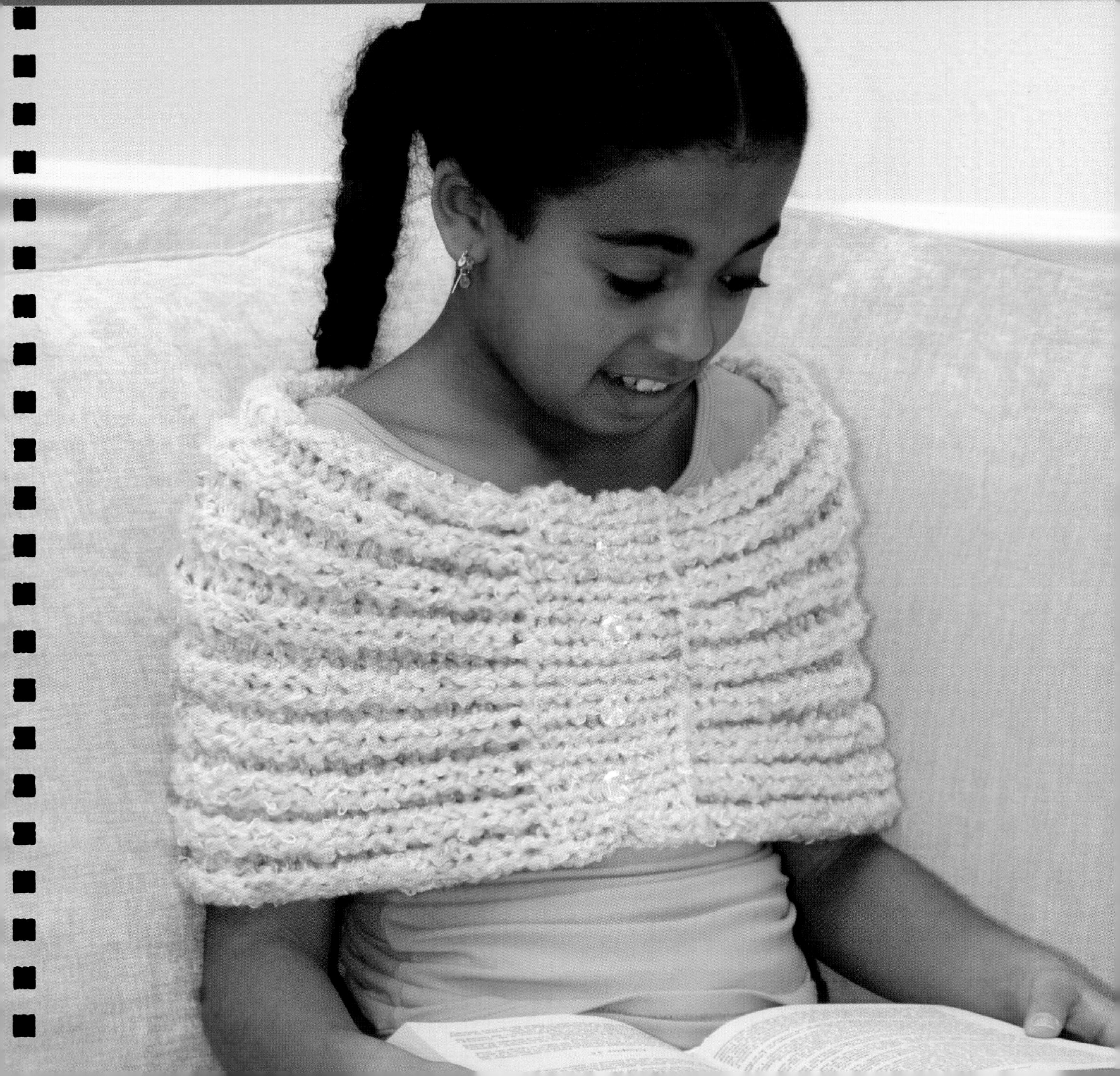

Scarf & Hat

Scarf Instructions

1. Start with ribbed stitch and knit five rows one-over-one on yellow loom.

2. Switch direction of knitting by using interrupted ribbed stitch. For five rows you will be interrupting normal ribbed stitch by wrapping loom across where you went in for two rows. Then you will switch back to way you wound the loom with ribbed stitch for one row, then you will switch back to other direction again for two more rows. This creates appearance of two small circles.

3. You will then switch back to ribbed stitch for five rows and continue this pattern until scarf is 55" long. Make sure to end on a section of ribbed stitch like beginning of knitting (there should be 43 sections of five rows each).

4. To sew scarf off loom, take yarn needle and sew through each loop twice before you remove it from loom. This will prevent scarf from gathering at end.

Hat Instructions

1. Start with ribbed stitch and knit 20 rows or 4" of knitting on blue loom using one-over-one stitch. This will form band on hat when folded up.

2. Knit 4½" more using combination of five rows of interrupted ribbed stitch (see description above) and five rows of ribbed stitch.

3. When knitting reaches 8½", cut yarn with enough left over to gather top together and sew down side of hat. Use yarn needle to sew through all loops in order from beginning loop to end loop.

Techniques
Ribbed stitch (see page 7)
Interrupted ribbed stitch (see page 9)
Mattress seam (see page 17)
One over-one stitch (see page 3)

Materials Needed
Knifty Knitter® Long Loom—Yellow
Knifty Knitter Long Loom—Blue
1 skein light-colored yarn

LIGHT 1 skein darker-colored yarn
Yarn needle

I used:
1 skein of Bernat® Baby Coordinates, Light (6 oz/170g), #01010 Soft Mauve
1 skein of Bernat® Baby Coordinates, Light (6 oz/170g), #01008 Baby Pink

Tip: If you use bulky weight yarn, you only need to use 1 strand of yarn at a time using the one-over-one stitch. If you use standard yarns like the weight listed above, treat the two strands of yarn as one strand and knit using the one-over-one stitch.

Finished Size
Scarf: 55" long
Hat: 8½" tall

Remove knitting from loom and gather loops tightly together. Sew down side of hat using mattress seam.

4. Fold up 2" of hat to form band. If desired, secure band down to hat using yarn, beads, jewels, or buttons.

5. Use Knifty Knitter® Pom-Pom & Tassel Maker to add pom-pom to top if desired.

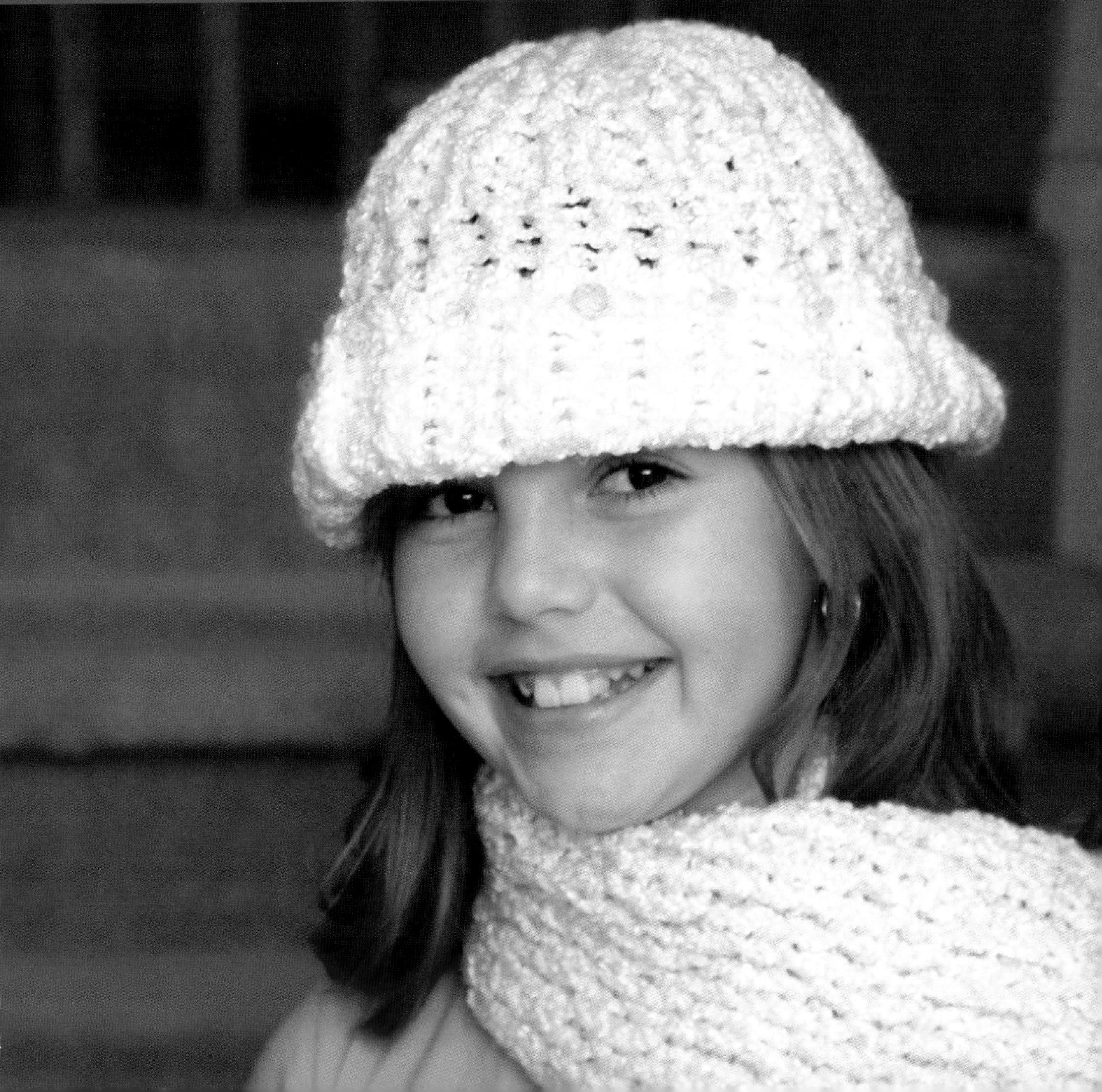

Prairie Scarf & Hat

Scarf Instructions

1. Use ribbed stitch to knit five rows of golden yarn on pink loom using one-over-one stitch.

2. Change color to multicolored yarn for bulk of scarf, and then change color back to golden yarn at end for five rows. Length of scarf is up to you, but it should be about 55" long.

3. Use Pom-Pom & Tassel Maker to make tassels using yarn of choice. Attach tassels to both ends of scarf.

Hat Instructions

1. Use ribbed stitch and one-over-one stitch on blue loom for two rows (or basically first winding of loom and knitting off) in golden yarn.

2. Change colors and knit remainder of hat in multicolored yarn until hat is 8½" long (you can make it ½" longer if you wish to cover ears better).

3. When you reach desired length of hat, cut yarn with enough left over to gather top together and sew down side of hat. Use yarn needle to sew through all loops in order from beginning loop to end loop, remove knitting from loom and gather loops tightly together. Sew down side of hat using mattress seam.

4. Fold up 2" of hat to form band. If desired, secure band down to hat using yarn, beads, jewels, or buttons.

5. Use Pom-Pom & Tassel Maker to add pom-pom to top if desired.

Techniques
Ribbed stitch (see page 7)
One-over-one stitch (see page 3)
Changing colors (see page 13)
Mattress seam (see page 17)

Materials Needed
Knifty Knitter® Long Loom—Pink
Knifty Knitter Long Loom—Blue
Knifty Knitter Pom-Pom & Tassel Maker
1 skein golden bulky yarn
1 skein multicolored bulky yarn
Yarn needle

BULKY 5

I used:
1 skein Lion Brand® Homespun®, Bulky (6 oz/170g), #790-380 Fawn
1 skein Lion Brand® Homespun®, Bulky (6 oz/170g), #790-335 Prairie

Tip: You will be using the ribbed stitch throughout the scarf and hat. The length of the use of the golden color is up to you (I used 5 rows on the scarf and 2 rows on the hat); just make sure you use the same amount on the other end of the scarf as well.

Finished Size
Scarf: 55" long
Hat: 8" tall

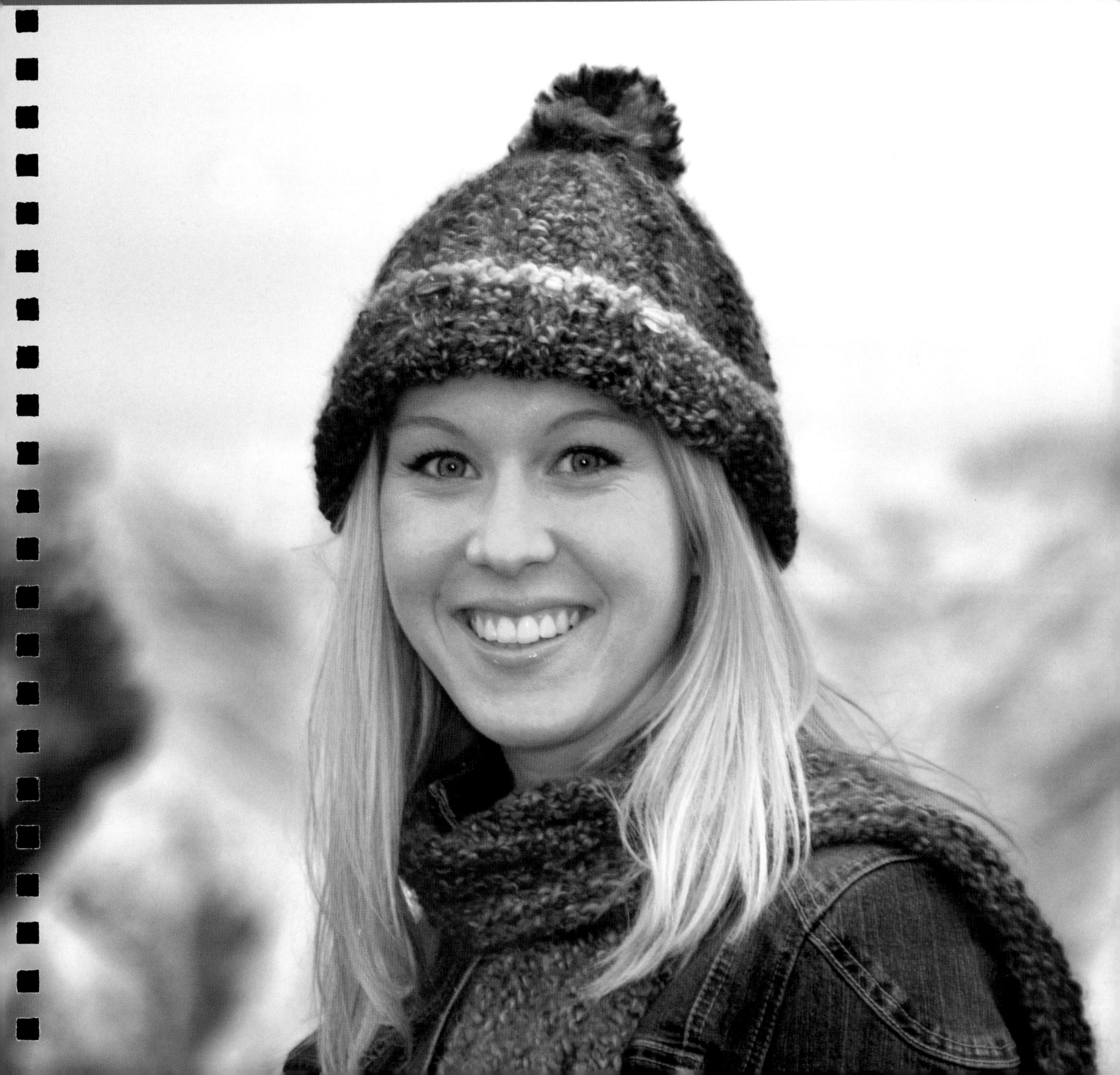

Afghan **Shawl**

Instructions

1. Tube knit with one-over-two stitch around entire loom until you have 2½" of knitting.

2. Decrease knitting on end/corner pegs at both ends until you are only using pegs across from one another.

3. Knit using ribbed stitch using one-over-one stitch until you have 48" of knitting.

4. Increase end/corner pegs back on as you begin to tube knit again for another 2½" of knitting using one-over-two stitch.

5. Sew each end of knitting with mattress seam to close 2½" tube knitted sections.

6. Add tassels to ends. You can purchase tassels, make them with beads, or make them on Pom-Pom & Tassel Maker using same yarn as afghan shawl.

Techniques
Tube knitting (see page 4)
Ribbed stitch (see page 7)
One-over-one stitch (see page 3)
One-over-two stitch (see page 3)
Decreasing (see page 12)
Increasing (see page 11)
Mattress seam (see page 17)

Materials Needed
Knifty Knitter® Long Loom—Blue
3 skeins multicolored bulky yarn
4 tassels
Yarn needle

I used:
3 skeins Lion Brand® Homespun®,
Bulky (6 oz/17g), #335 Prairie
4 tassels Wrights® Home Collection
Tassels 2" (50.8 mm), #1444040560

Finished Size
15" x 48"

Mommy & Me
Blanket

This blanket can be used while they are babies in your arms, all the way up through their teen years.

Instructions

To make this large blanket, create three long panels with three colored squares each on blue loom. Colored squares in this example use two different colored yarn threads at one time (you can choose to use any color or weight yarn you prefer to match your room). Both small color threads were treated as one thread and knitted one-over-one using ribbed stitch and interrupted ribbed stitch.

1. Take two threads of yarn that you will be using and create loop with both yarns in order to hold it down on first peg—or simply secure it in place as you begin winding so that it doesn't come undone. You will be repeating pattern of five knitted rows of ribbed stitch, then five rows of interrupted ribbed stitch. As you use two knitting stitches, you will notice pattern that resembles circles. Quick visual guide is that each color square will need to be 15 diagonal circles wide and 15 circles long (it is much easier than

continued on page 52

Techniques
Ribbed stitch (see page 7)
Interrupted ribbed stitch (see page 9)
One-over-one stitch (see page 3)
Color changing (see page 13)
Mattress seam (see page 17)

Materials Needed
Knifty Knitter® Long Loom—Blue
2 skeins light blue yarn
2 skeins light purple yarn
2 skeins light pink yarn
2 skeins white yarn
2 skeins light green yarn
1 skein light yellow yarn
Yarn needle

LIGHT 3

I used:
2 skeins Bernat® Baby Coordinates, Light (6 oz/170g), #01009 Soft Blue
2 skeins Bernat® Baby Coordinates, Light (6 oz/170g), #01010 Soft Mauve
2 skeins Bernat® Baby Coordinates, Light (6 oz/170g), #01008 Baby Pink
2 skeins Bernat® Baby Coordinates, Light (6 oz/170g), #01000 White
2 skeins Bernat® Baby Coordinates, Light (6 oz/170g), #01012 Iced Mint
1 skein Bernat® Baby Coordinates, Light (6 oz/170g), #01011 Lemon Custard

Finished Size
Fits twin bed
Tip: You can always add more panels to make the blanket larger.

Mommy & Me
Blanket continued

counting 75 rows per color square) or that you will be making 15 direction changes every five rows.

2. When you reach end of colored square, you will just wind two new color threads and continue pattern as usual. Make sure each square is same length so panels line up correctly.

3. When you reach end of long panel, use yarn needle to sew through each loop twice before you remove it from loom. This will help prevent knit from gathering together.

4. When all three long panels are knitted, sew panels together with mattress seam. Make sure you have each panel on right side (if you look closely you will see difference from one side of knitting to other). Secure all loose ends or areas where you made a color change with square knots and hide thread in knitting.

Color Combinations
Used for this Blanket Example

Left side panel: Light green yarn was used with light yellow yarn for first square, light purple yarn with white yarn for middle square, and pink yarn with pink yarn

for last square (FYI: This is because pink disappears next to other colors and I wanted a pink square in my blanket).

Middle panel: Light blue yarn with light green yarn for first square, light yellow yarn with light pink yarn for middle square, and light purple yarn with light blue yarn for last square.

Right side panel: Light pink yarn with light purple yarn for first square, light blue yarn with white yarn for middle square, and light green yarn with white yarn for last square.

Smaller Blanket Option

You can also choose to make a smaller blanket like baby blanket shown here. This blanket used baby yarns of yellow with white yarn and blue with green yarn. Simply choose your two favorite color combinations and make two panels of two color squares like blanket pictured at right. Sew two panels together with mattress seam, and then sew ribbon that matches between each color change and/or sew or tie on bows to middle, ends, or corners if desired.

Baseball & Basketball
Pillows

Other possibilities with this pattern are tennis balls, apples, tomatoes, pumpkins, or funky disco balls.

Instructions

1. Tube knit around entire green loom using one-over-two stitch to create 12" long tube.

2. Thread yarn needle and sew through loops on loom. Remove tube from loom and gently pull and gather loops together. Since yarn is bulky, you will not be able to gather ball completely together so you will need to sew hole closed, knot securely, and hide thread inside ball.

3. Turn ball inside out if desired (leave as is if you prefer ribbed pattern on outside). Stuff ball using fiberfill or cluster stuffing (which would be softer, but wouldn't hold ball shape as well). To use fiberfill, cut batting into long 3" strips. Roll batting as you would create yarn ball, rolling different directions to form general ball shape. Cut more 3" strips and wrap them around ball until ball is right size for ball tube.

4. Stuff tube and then use yarn needle to gather all loops on bottom together. Sew remaining hole together, knot, and hide remaining thread in ball pillow.
continued on page 56

Techniques
Tube knitting (see page 4)
One-over-two stitch (see page 3)

Materials Needed
Knifty Knitter® Long Loom—Green
3 skeins white bulky yarn or 3 skeins orange bulky yarn
1 skein red bulky yarn or 1 skein black bulky yarn
Fiberfill or cluster stuffing
Clear adhesive tape
Black sewing thread or embroidery floss
Sewing needle
Yarn needle

I used:
For the baseball:
3 skeins Moda Dea™ Aerie™, Bulky (1¾ oz/50g), #9113 Ecru
1 skein Moda Dea™ Aerie™, Bulky (1¾ oz/50g), #9390 Red

For the basketball:
3 skeins Moda Dea™ Aerie™, Bulky (1¾ oz/50g), #9277 Coral
1 skein Lion Brand® Wool-Ease® Chunky, Bulky (5 oz/14g), #630-153 Black

Finished Size
9" round

Tip: When creating baseball and basketball it is easier to have real ball or picture to copy lines and patterns on ball.

Creating the Baseball Lines

1. Lay out pattern on ball using clear adhesive tape to achieve swirling circle pattern. You will be sewing over top of tape to create even stitches.

2. Use red bulky yarn and yarn needle to sew small even stitches vertically over top of tape pattern you placed around entire ball. Secure red yarn with knot and hide ends in ball. Gently remove and cut away tape pattern.

3. Once tape is removed, use red yarn again and sew straight horizontal lines through stitched lines around entire ball (creating illusion that 2 pieces were stitched together to form baseball).

Creating the Basketball Lines

1. Wrap basketball like gift using black bulky yarn. Take yarn and wrap it from top to bottom of ball, twist and then wrap yarn coming back up on left and right side of ball. Knot thread together, and use yarn needle to hide strings inside basketball.

2. Use black thread or embroidery floss to sew over top and under black yarn lines to secure them in place.

3. To create swirling circle pattern, lay pattern out with black yarn 1" away from where yarn crossed in middle of ball. Adjust yarn as you sew it down so it is centered between lines as you go around ball. When you reach starting point again with black thread, knot yarn and hide thread in ball.

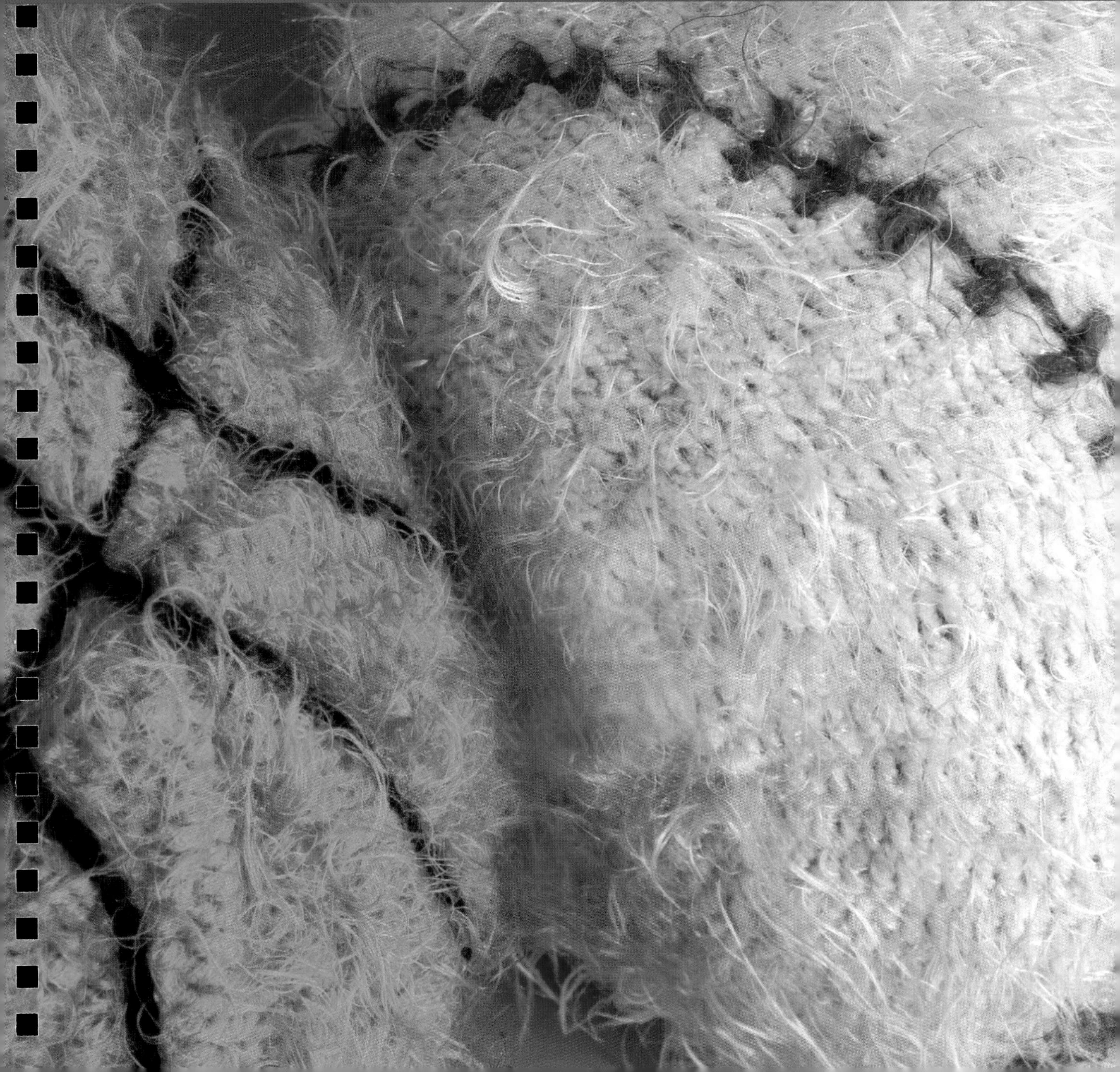

Let's play

Explore a new level of knitting with the exciting projects in this section, and have some fun while you're at it! These one-of-a-kind toys and costumes are just a few ways you can play with the Knifty Knitter® looms. With projects for pirates, princesses, cowboys, and more, let your imagination bring your clever creations to life!

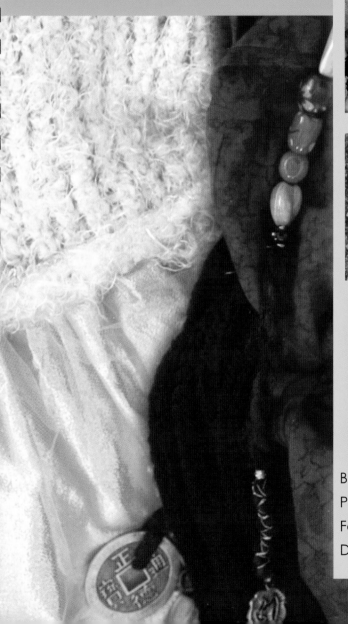

Broom
Horse

Instructions

1. Tube knit on pink loom 23" long tube using brown yarn. Use yarn needle to gather loops together. Knot and hide thread in snout (gathered end).

2. Place plastic bag over top of broom and secure bag with twine to broom handle. Pull tube over broom, put in ball of fiberfill or loose ball of yarn at end of broom to form snout, and secure bottom of tube by tying twine around outside of tube and broom handle.

3. For nosepiece, create 10" I-cord using black yarn. Sew two ends of I-cord together to form circle. Place nosepiece vertically between ball of stuffing and broom bristles.

4. Create 7" long black I-cord and tie this horizontally into nosepiece across front to create mouthpiece.

5. Create rein by braiding three 30" lengths of twine together. Attach rein to each side of horse's head where you attached mouthpiece by pushing twine through and tying square knot.

continued on page 62

Techniques
Tube knitting (see page 4)
I-cord (see page 6)
Mattress seam (see page 17)
Two-over-two stitch (see page 3)

Materials Needed
Knifty Knitter® Long Loom—Pink
1 skein brown medium yarn
1 skein black bulky yarn
MEDIUM 4
Angle broom
Plastic bag
Twine
Sewing thread and needle
Yarn needle
Crochet hook
Loose ball of fiberfill or yarn
2 sets of buttons (for eyes)
BULKY 5
Vinyl or felt (for ear)

I used:
1 skein Lion Brand® Wool-Ease®, Medium (3 oz/85g), #620-125 Camel
1 skein Lion Brand® Wool-Ease® Chunky, Bulky (5 oz/14g), #630-153 Black

Finished Size
14" head

Broom
Horse continued

6. Use any loom to make the ears (see picture to right). Use four pegs and panel knit four rows. Reduce end pegs to two rows. Reduce to one peg and pull thread through last loop and knot. Sew loose thread down side of ear and use same thread to sew ear on horse. You can also create ears by cutting vinyl or felt in shape of ear. Sew ear on using mattress seam when adding mane.

shape for felt ear

7. Create mane across top and down back of horse by using black yarn and wrapping it 10 times around your fingers. Cut strand of black yarn and tie it around one end of wrapped yarn (see illustration). Take tied bundle and using crochet hook, thread knotted yarn ends through each side of knitted row at top of horse. Tie threads together with square knot (see red circled knots in photo to right). Create two of these bundles facing toward nose about three to four knitted rows apart. Sew ears on and

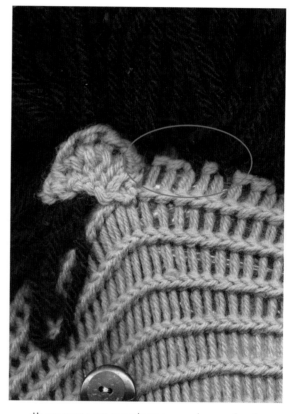

then sew on neck mane pieces facing broom handle. Make these longer by wrapping them around palm of hand. Sew on as many bundles as you like to create desired look.

8. Sew on two button eyes in same place on either side of head.

Costume & Boots
Pirate

Techniques
I-cord (see page 6)
Tube knitting (see page 4)
One-over-one stitch (see page 3)

Materials Needed: Hairpiece
Knifty Knitter® Long Loom—Yellow
1 skein black bulky yarn
1 skein black/brown bulky yarn
¼ yard material in red or with pirate
theme
Beads and pendants
Yarn needle
Needle and thread

I used:
1 skein Lion Brand® Woolease ®, Thick &
Quick®, (6 oz/170g), #153 Black
1 skein Lion Brand® Woolease®, Thick &
Quick®, (6 oz/170g), #426 Cabin Brown
The Dress It Up Bead Company®, Special
Selection®, color coordinated glass
beads, #13
The Beadery Craft Products®, elements®,
Beads and Accessories, Painted
Wooden Beads Mix, Purple Hibiscus,
#1416H
& Asian Dragon Pendants, antique silver,
#2646H

Finished Size
Fit hairpiece to any size head

Instructions for Pirate Hairpiece

1. You will first need to create cap piece to sew dreadlocks onto. Use yellow long loom. Tube knit on yellow loom with brown/black yarn using a one-over-one stitch. Create a 6" long tube, take yarn needle and sew through loops left on loom, remove loops, and gather together tightly and knot. This will be shorter than most hats so it will not show under material.

2. Create several I-cords that will be sewn onto cap piece to look like dreadlocks. For bangs or front of hairpiece, create three black I-cords that are 20" long, and two black/brown I-cords that are 20" long. For back of head, create 12 black I-cords that are 36" long, and six black/brown I-cords that are 36" long. Be sure to knot ends of I-cords and to cut excess thread.

3. Create 36" long string (use thread or yarn) of various sized beads. Add medallion or heavy metal disk at each end. This will be sewn on with I-cords as decoration. You can also create additional strings of beads and add them throughout dreadlocks.

4. Using yarn and yarn needle, you will be tacking down shorter I-cords to cap piece. Start sewing at gathering point *continued on page 64*

Costume & Boots
Pirate continued

or top of cap piece. Fold each 20" long I-cord in half and begin tacking these I-cords down at their fold point with black I-cords underneath and black/brown I-cords on top. This will give hair appearance of highlights. Then sew on 36" string of beads to front of cap piece.

5. For longer I-cords you will start tacking I-cords down back of cap piece. Fold each longer I-cord in half, and first sew black I-cords down back of cap piece at their fold point. Next, sew black/brown I-cords on top of longer black I-cords to act as hair highlights. Add additional beads if desired.

6. Put on cap piece and then take ¼ yard of material (folded so you do not see raw edges) and tie it around front of cap piece (which has no I-cords), under dreadlocks, and knot it at back of neck.

Instructions for Pirate Boots

1. Tube knit using one-over-one stitch for 85 rows or 40" long. Take yarn needle and sew through loops, remove loops from loom, and gather tightly together and knot. Hide thread in boot. Then create second boot same way.

2. Fold top of each yarn boot down about 2" or more to form cuff on boot.

Materials Needed: Boots
Knifty Knitter Long® Loom—Pink
1 skein brown or black bulky yarn
4 large antique gold or silver buttons
Yarn needle
Needle and thread

BULKY 5

I used:
1 skein Lion Brand® Chunky Woolease®, (5 oz/140g), #127 Walnut

Finished Size
This will fit up to man's size 9

Note: Make boot longer for larger foot. For children's feet, use Knifty Knitter® Flower Loom and adjust length to child's foot and calf.

Pinch cuff together at top and sew two large buttons together on each side of cuff about ½" from edge. This will help tighten top of boot so it will stay up on calf.

3. You can place these boots over shoes or sew on thick material piece to bottom to make boots thicker to wear without shoes.

4. Stuff pants into boots and make sure buttons are on outside of each leg.

Additional costume items:
White/cream long sleeve shirt
Black/brown/or tan long pants
Scarves to wrap around waist
Plastic sword or pistol

Fancy Dress-Up

Any creative color combinations can be used, including white for a bride's dress-up gown or more casual material combinations to create a nice dress to wear.

Instructions for Making the Dress

1. Tube knit on green loom using one-over-one stitch for 10 rows.

2. Decrease end/corner pegs so that you will now create an opening for sleeves.

3. Continue knitting on one side of loom (or 24 pegs) by panel knitting for another 28 rows. Cut and knot yarn, but do not remove knitting from loom. Take thread of bright yarn and sew through five pegs on one end of 24 pegs and then do same on other side to create shoulder connections. Gently remove these loops from loom. With yarn needle, sew off remaining loops from loom by securing yarn to knitting and sewing twice through each loop of 14 remaining loops, knotting and securing knitting again. This will be neck opening in back of dress.

4. Begin panel knitting on other side of loom (or 24 pegs) to create front of the dress. Knit 15 rows.

5. To create neck and shoulders of dress you will be sewing off 14 of middle loops and knitting on five pegs at each end of 24 pegs. To do this, take yarn needle and *continued on page 68*

continued on page 68

Techniques
One-over-one stitch (see page 3)
Tube knitting (see page 4)
Panel knitting (see page 5)
Decreasing (see page 12)
Increasing (see page 11)
Mattress seam (see page 17)
Hidden seam (see page 18)
I-cord (see page 6)

Materials Needed
Knifty Knitter® Long Loom—Green
2 skeins super bulky/furry yarn
1 yard silver material
1 yard blue netting material
½" thick silver lace
(2 packages or 4 yards)
Yarn needle
Needle and thread

SUPER BULKY 6

Note: Standard weight yarns will not work with this pattern.

I used:
2 skeins Patons® Allure, Super Bulky
(1¾ oz/50g), #04128 Aquamarine

Finished Size
Sizes 12–24 months

Fancy Dress-Up *continued*

thread, knot it securely to knitting five pegs in, and begin sewing through each of 14 loops twice and removing them from loom. Do not sew off five pegs on other end of 24 pegs. Knot securely to knitting. Panel knit on five pegs at each end for 13 more rows to create shoulder pieces.

6. Use bright piece of yarn to sew through five shoulder loops on one side, and then repeat on other shoulder (this will prevent loops from pulling through when you create hidden seams). Gently remove loops from loom.

7. Place two right sides of shoulder together and sew them together with hidden seam.

8. To create arms, panel knit on 24 pegs (or one side of green loom) for 10 rows. Reduce two end pegs and knit on 22 pegs for two rows. Continue this pattern of knitting two rows and reducing end pegs until you have 12 pegs left. Knit final two rows on 12 pegs and then remove loops from loom by sewing through each loop twice and removing it from loom.

9. Use mattress seam to sew up each arm and to sew arms to openings in dress.

10. Take yard of silver material and blue netting material and fold both in half lengthwise with right sides of material together. Cut both in half on this fold. With sewing machine or by hand, sew down each short side of lengthwise panel. This tube will be bottom of dress. Hem bottom if necessary.

Note: Netting material does not need to be hemmed, and if you're lucky some materials like the silver material I used do not need to be hemmed because of the way they were finished on the sellvage.

11. With needle and thread, baste top of material tube in order to gently gather material together. Pin this gathered skirt onto knitted top and sew them together.

12. Sew silver lace by hand around each arm, around neck, and around waist of dress. This helps to strengthen edges of knitting.

Instructions for Making the Hat

1. Use 18 pegs on one side of loom and panel knit using one-over-one stitch for five rows.

2. Decrease two end pegs and panel knit for five rows on 16 pegs.

3. Repeat this pattern of knitting five rows and decreasing two ends until you are down to last two pegs.

4. Knit one loop over other and take working yarn through last loop, pull, and knot to remove from loom.

5. Repeat steps 1–4 to create another side, and then sew two sides of triangle together using mattress seam. Leave bottom of triangle open to add cone.

6. To create cone, use two sheets of cardstock laying horizontally to create two loose funnels that you will staple together to create one funnel that will fit top of your child's head. Place cardboard funnel inside knitted hat. Secure yarn to cardboard at bottom with thread and needle or with glue.

7. Create an I-cord that can be sewn or glued to bottom edge of hat. Add silver lace above I-cord with glue or thread.

Materials Needed
Knifty Knitter® Long Loom— Yellow
(or any loom with 18 pegs)
1 skein super bulky furry yarn
¼ yard more silver material
or silver ribbon
¼ yard blue netting material
Silver lace
 2 sheets of cardstock
Fabric glue
Yarn needle
Needle and thread
Optional: I glued on silver stars to the outside of the hat and down the blue netting material

I used:
1 skein Patons® Allure, Super Bulky
(1¾ oz/50g), #04128 Aquamarine

8. Create streamers of material (silver and blue netting material) or use wide ribbons that you will gently push through top of cone and knot inside hat.

9. Sew on ribbon or elastic or use bobby pins to secure hat on head. You can also glue on silver stars to knitted hat and to blue netting material for extra sparkle.

Black and White Dress Option

Different Materials Needed
2 skeins bulky yarn
Black and white material
½" thick black lace
3 white artificial daisies (2 more for decoration on the shoes)
3 black buttons (2 more for the shoes)
1 yard white silk ribbon (bow used under middle front daisy)

I used:
2 skeins Bernat® Baby Lash, Bulky (1.75oz/50g), #67005 Wee White

I followed fancy dress-up pattern instructions, only I hemmed bottom of dress higher and added some different embellishments.

Note: To create flower embellishments, simply remove petal grouping from wire stem and use needle and thread to sew black button and petals onto dress. A bow of white silk ribbon can also be sewn underneath daisy.

Dice with
Family Games

Instructions

1. Tube knit around entire pink loom with one-over-two stitch (to make it thicker) until you form 6" tube. When completed, take yarn needle and sew through each loop twice before you remove it from loom to prevent tube from gathering together when removing.

2. Keep plastic packaging on block so tube will slide on block easier. You may want to cover bright colors on packaging that may show through white knitting with square of white paper.

3. Use eight pegs on pink loom and panel knit until you have 6" long piece. You will create two of these end pieces. Make sure you sew through each loop twice as you remove them from loom to prevent panel from gathering together. Sew end pieces on with mattress seam around entire outside of block.

Tip: You may have gaps created when you sew around block and pull knitting together. A trick to cover these gaps is to sew a straight line through knitted loops to create illusion of a replacement row for row that was pulled together when sewing.

continued on page 72

Techniques
Tube knitting (see page 4)
Panel knitting (see page 5)
One-over-two stitch (see page 3)
Mattress seam (see page 17)

Materials Needed
Knifty Knitter® Long Loom—Pink
1 skein white bulky yarn
21 black buttons ½" or 1" wide
4 " square styrofoam block (usually found in floral departments)
Black thread and sewing needle
Yarn needle

BULKY 5

I used:
1 skein Bernat® Baby Lash, Bulky (1 ¾ oz/50g), #67005 Wee White
I also suggest: 1 skein Patons® Allure, Bulky (1 ¾ oz/50g), #04005 Diamond

Finished Size
About 5" cube

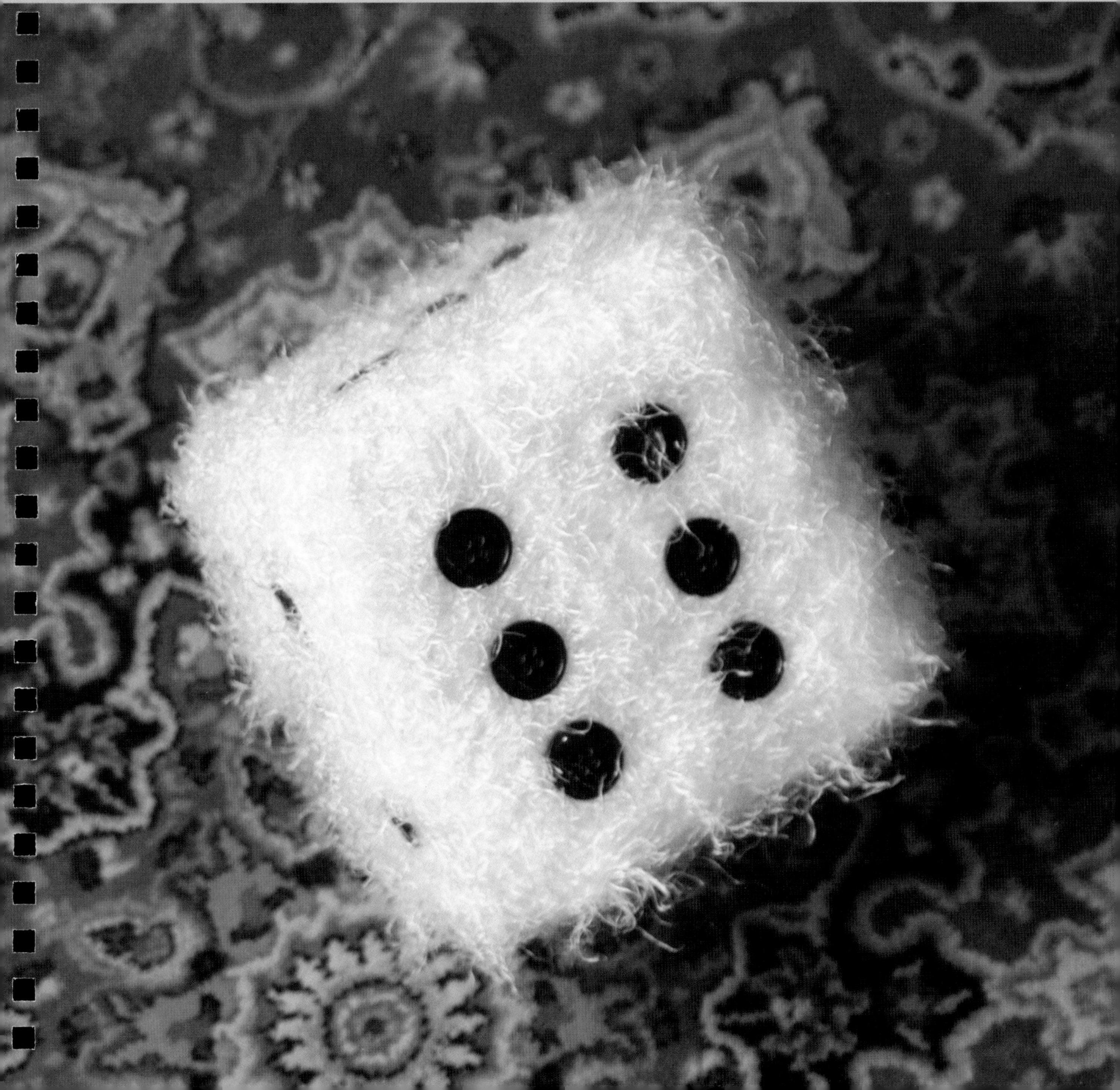

Dice with
Family Games *continued*

4. Sew 21 buttons on appropriate sides with black thread (have die handy to look at and copy). To keep buttons even, place tape measure on one corner and extend to opposite corner of block. This gives diagonal path to place buttons evenly under for numbers 2, 3, and 5. Tape measure also helps to center and create lines to place buttons under for numbers 1, 4, and 6.

Uses for the Dice

Besides using as a game replacement to make the standard family game a little more fun, you can also use the dice for a math practice game or a "getting to know you" better game.

Math Practice Game

See how many rolls you and your children can add or multiply together before you can't go any further. The number of rolls becomes the score of the person. The first person to some designated number wins. It helps to have a calculator nearby to check your answers if they get too high.

Getting to Know You Better Game

Take turns having everyone in the room roll the die and answer the corresponding question to the number they land on. The number of the die becomes their score and the first one to 20 or a designated number wins.

Questions for the die numbers

1. Name something you don't like. (Not people)

2. Name something you like. (Such as food, behavior, color, sport, day of the week, etc.)

3. Name something you want to do or somewhere you want to go.

4. Tell about a good experience you have had or tell about someone you admire.

5. Tell about something interesting you have learned or something you would like to learn.

6. Tell about a goal you have set for yourself or tell about an embarrassing moment.

Family crafts

Have some family fun with these Knifty Knitter® crafts designed just for you and your loved ones. There's something for everyone, whether you want to surprise the outdoorsy boy, provide a project for the fashion-forward girl, or dress up a gift for the holidays. Everyone in the family can take part in making something with the Knifty Knitter looms. These creative projects are unlike anything else you've knitted before, so pick a pattern and get started!

Journal
Book Covers

Instructions

1. Tube knit around entire pink loom until you have 9" long tube.

Tip: Make sure that this size fits journal or book you are covering. You may also want to use larger looms if your journal is larger.

2. Knit on one side of pink loom only by panel knitting for five rows.

3. You will need to sew twice through each loop or crochet off loops on opposite side of loom (side you did not panel knit on) to form first journal pocket.

4. Go back to side you panel knitted on and begin increasing by wrapping around entire loom again so you can tube knit. Tube knit around entire loom again to create another 9" long tube.

5. You will need to sew closed both ends of knitting with mattress seam to finish off both end pockets. Tie a knot when you finish sewing and hide thread inside journal pocket.

6. Stuff ribbon in middle front of cover for ties (make sure ribbon is secured to cover with sewing thread and buttons), or add twine by taking loop up through bottom pocket and threading yarn through it and pulling. If desired, add beads, jewels, buttons, squares of material, or any embellishment you wish to make journal or book cover personal.

Techniques
Tube knitting (see page 4)
Panel knitting (see page 5)
Increasing (see page 11)
Mattress seam (see page 17)

Materials Needed
Knifty Knitter® Long Loom—Pink
1 skein bulky or super bulky yarn
Ribbon or twine for ties
(approximately ½ yard)
Decorative buttons or leather/material
squares (optional)
Yarn needle

SUPER BULKY 6

I used:
1 skein Lion Brand® Homespun®, Bulky
(6 oz/170g), #790-370 Coral Gables
1 skein Lion Brand® Wool-Ease®
Thick & Quick®, Super Bulky
(6 oz/170g), #640-131 Grass

Finished Size
Depending on journal or book; I made covers 7" x 9"

7. In one side of journal or book cover you should be able to place your book or journal. In the other side you can put in crayons, colored pencils, stickers, or mementoes.

Tip: For outdoor journal or book, you can add pocketknife, compass, first aid kit, or flashlight. Then flip journal cover over your belt, tie it closed, and take it with you hiking.

Girls Sleepover
Crafts

Socks Instructions

1. Knit 12" long tube on Flower Loom with one-over-one stitch.

2. Sew with yarn needle through each loop on loom. Remove from loom, gather, and knot. Turn inside out. Create two.

Hair Scrunchies Instructions

1. Tube knit on Flower Loom using one-over-one stitch, except wrap loom with e-wraps on inside. It helps if you turn the slits in the pegs to inside.

2. Knit six rows. Place hair elastic around pegs in middle of the six rows.

3. Place bottom loops back on loom and knit. Sew with yarn needle twice through each loop left on loom and then knot and remove hair scrunchy from loom.

Boa or Scarf Instructions

1. Tube knit around entire Flower Loom with one-over-one stitch until scarf has reached desired length of about 50" long.

2. Sew with yarn needle up through each loop and around through loop again to secure loops before removing from loom.

3. Turn scarf inside out to furry side if desired. You can knot ends of scarf to weight them.

Socks Techniques
Tube knitting (see page 4)
One-over-one stitch (see page 3)
Materials Needed
Knifty Knitter® Flower Loom
2 skeins blue bulky yarn, Yarn needle
I used:
2 skeins Bernat® Baby Lash, Bulky
(1¾ oz/50g), #67143 Bunny Blue

Finished Size
About 12" long

Hair Scrunchies Techniques
Tube knitting (see page 4)
One-over-one stitch (see page 3)
Materials Needed
Knifty Knitter® Flower Loom
1 skein bulky yarn, Hair elastic, Yarn needle
I used:
1 skein Bernat® Baby Lash, Bulky
(1¾ oz/50g), #67143 Bunny Blue

Finished Size
1" thick band

Boa or Scarf Techniques
Tube knitting (see page 4)
One-over-one stitch (see page 3)
Materials Needed
Knifty Knitter® Flower Loom
1 skein bulky yarn, Yarn needle
I used:
1 skein Bernat® Disco, Bulky (1¾ oz/50g),
#68728 Fuchsia Fever for boa
Or 1 skein Lion Brand® Homespun® Baby,
Bulky (3 oz/85g), #800-101 Pink Carnation
for scarf

Finished Size
About 50" long

Bird *Marionette*

Instructions

1. Using one-over-two stitch to make bird body very furry, tube knit 4" tube on Flower Loom using light blue yarn. Sew through remaining loops on loom, remove from loom with yarn needle, and gather top loops tightly together and knot. Turn inside out and place on styrofoam ball. With long strand of yarn and yarn needle, gather bottom of tube loops together tightly and knot. You will use this long yarn strand to attach neck piece on to bird's body later.

2. Create 2" long I-cord with blue yarn. Thread I-cord onto long thread from body. This will be bird's neck.

3. For head, tube knit 2" tube with blue yarn using one-over-two stitch. Sew through loops on loom, gather, and knot securely. Turn inside out and stuff head with fiberfill stuffing or cotton balls. Sew and gather other end tightly together. With yarn needle, thread long yarn strand from neck piece through head and secure with knot. For face, glue or sew on eyes, and add square yellow foam or felt folded to form triangle beak.
continued on page 82

Techniques
Tube knitting (see page 4)
One-over-two stitch (see page 3)
I-cord (see page 6)

Materials Needed
Knifty Knitter® Flower Loom
Knifty Knitter Pom-Pom & Tassel Maker
1 skein blue bulky/furry yarn
1 skein green bulky/furry yarn
2 styrofoam balls (3" size)
Fiberfill stuffing or cotton balls
Fishing line
2 chopsticks, skewers, or wooden sticks
2 google eyes or buttons
1¼" square yellow foam or felt
Glue
Yarn needle

I used:
1 skein Bernat® Baby Lash, Bulky
(1¾ oz/50g), #67143 Bunny Blue
1 skein Red Heart® Foxy™, Bulky
(1¾ oz/50g), #9630 Grass

Note: If you use standard weight yarn you will need to create a lining and a cover piece to prevent the styrofoam ball from showing through. Just make the cover piece two rows bigger than the size of your original knitted piece and add this cover on top of the lining. I suggest you also use the two-over-two stitch to make it thick enough.

Finished Size
15" tall bird

Bird *Marionette* *continued*

4. For feet, saw or carefully cut one styrofoam ball in half. Knit two 3" tubes using one-over-two stitch and green yarn. For each tube you create, sew through and gather top and knot securely. Turn each tube inside out, add half styrofoam ball, and gather bottom loops of each foot tightly together and knot.

5. Create 10" long I-cord out of green yarn for legs. Make sure you have enough yarn on each end of I-cord to thread through each foot. Thread yarn through center of one foot (cut-end of ball facing downward) and secure with knot. Take other end of I-cord and thread between knitted body and styrofoam ball at center bottom of bird body. Center I-cord so you have two 5" long legs. Thread end of I-cord through center of other foot and secure with knot.

6. Create green and blue pom-pom on Pom-Pom & Tassel Maker and attach to back of bird as tail.

7. Take two chopsticks or sticks and use fishing line to wind and wrap them together to form cross.

Tip: Cut grooves at end of each stick to hold fishing line in place or use glue gun to secure line to stick ends.

8. Cut one long string of fishing line. Take string of fishing line and tie it to bottom of cross. Use yarn needle to thread other end of string across top of body (but not into styrofoam ball), through neck, and out top of head. Wind and knot string to top of cross after adjusting marionette to desired look on string.

9. Cut two other strings of fishing line. You will attach and knot one string to top front of one foot and then wind and secure other end of string to side of cross, and other string on other foot and other side of cross.

10. Walk bird by rocking cross from side to side.

Worm Marionette

Instructions

1. Create lining and cover to prevent styrofoam ball from showing through standard or medium weight yarn. Four linings and four covers will need to be created by tube knitting with two-over-two stitch. For each lining create one 3" tube. Sew through and gather top, add styrofoam ball, sew through, and gather bottom of tube. For each cover create 4" tube and follow same instructions as above.

2. Cut long string of fishing line and tie it to one end of stick. Use yarn needle to thread line through center of gathering point of each tube, under knitting (but not into styrofoam ball), and out center of gathering point at other end of all four balls. Tie and secure string to other end of stick. Use glue gun or regular glue to secure fishing line to stick.

3. To decorate and add personality to worm, glue on eyes, attach small pom-pom nose using Pom-Pom & Tassel Maker, add glasses made from black pipe cleaner, and cut foam to add mouth and clothes such as bow tie and buttons.

4. To keep sections of worm together, tie each ball together with piece of yarn.

Techniques
Tube knitting (see page 4)
Two-over-two stitch (see page 3)

Materials Needed
Knifty Knitter® Flower Loom
Knifty Knitter Pom-Pom & Tassel Maker
1 skein medium weight yarn
4 styrofoam balls (3" size)
Fishing line
1 chopstick, skewer, or wooden stick
2 google eyes or buttons
Foam or felt in black and white
1 black pipe cleaner folded like glasses
Glue
Yarn needle

I used:
1 skein Red Heart® Super Saver™, Medium (7 oz/198g), #0672 Spring Green

Note: If you use bulky weight yarn that is furry you do not need to create a lining or cover. Just knit with a one-over–two stitch.

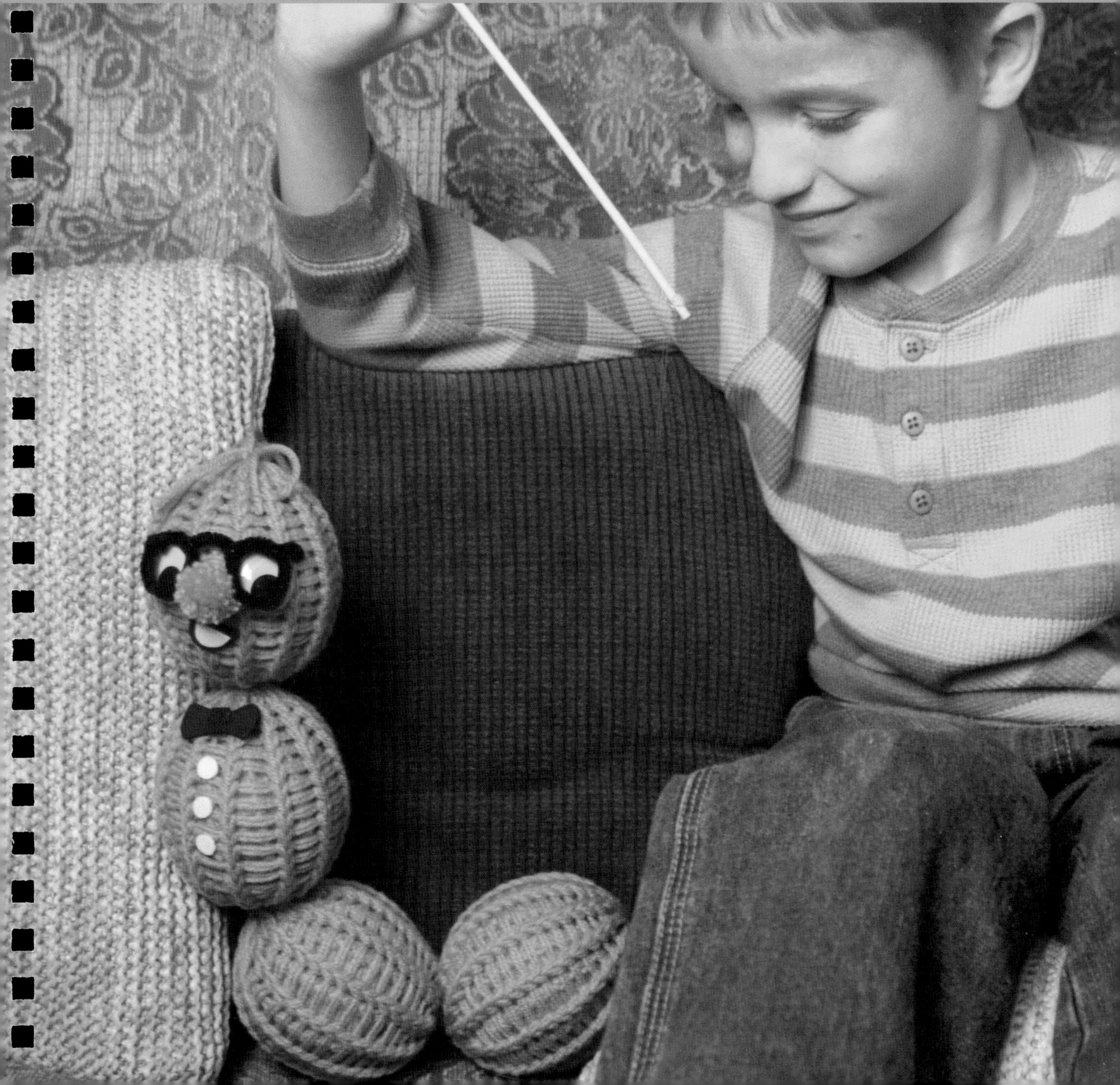

Have a Ball
Crafts

General Instructions

1. Tube knit 4" long tube on Flower Loom. Stitch you use depends on yarn choice. If you are using bulky or furry yarns you can use one-over-one stitch or one-over-two stitch (which makes it thicker). If you are using medium or standard weight yarn, you will need to create lining and cover to prevent stuffing or styrofoam from being seen through knitting. Lining should be 3" long tube that you cover and surround ball with first, and cover should be 4" long tube that you place on top and gather together.

2. Using yarn needle, sew through loops, remove tube from loom, and gather together. Turn tube inside out if desired.

3. Stuff styrofoam ball or stuffing material in tube. With yarn needle and yarn, gather all bottom loops together tightly, knot, and hide strings inside ball.

Ideas for the Balls

Christmas Ornaments

1. After creating your green or red balls, cut a length of ribbon 12" long or longer (if you use bigger beads you will

Techniques
Tube knitting (see page 4)

Materials Needed
Knifty Knitter® Flower Loom
1 skein bulky yarn
Or
1 skein medium or standard yarn
3" styrofoam balls
Yarn needle

Finished Size
3" round

Christmas Ornaments:
I used:
3" styrofoam balls
Ribbon and beads
1 skein No Boundaries®, Bulky (50g/30 m), #24 Stella
1 skein Red Heart® Foxy™, Bulky (1¾ oz/50g), #9630 Grass

need longer ribbon). Fold ribbon in half and add one to three beads to bottom and knot to hold beads in place.

continued on page 88

Have a Ball
Crafts *continued*

2. Take top loop of folded ribbon and thread in yarn needle. Thread yarn needle through bottom gathering point, around styrofoam ball under knitting, and out through top gathering point.

3. If desired, thread top of ribbon with beads. Use top loop to hang ornament on tree.

Dog and Cat Toys

1. Create ball, but make sure you stuff your ball with stuffing material—not styrofoam. Add rattle inside by taking bead and enclosing it in film container if desired.

2. To decorate create I-cords that are same length and attach them to bottom of ball. To create bird ball for cat, sew on eyes and square material beak, folded and sewn on its side to form beak.

Other Ball Craft Ideas

Special Occasion Ideas

You can also create apple pincushions, stuffed pumpkins, and ghost windsocks. The ideas are endless. Use google eyes, foam or felt, pipe cleaners, pom-poms, even shredded garbage bags for the windsock. Let your imagination run wild.

BULKY 5 *Dog and Cat Toys*: I used:
1 skein No Boundaries®, Bulky (50g/30 m), #24 Stella (dog toy)
Yarn in various colors for I-cords (dog toy)
Bernat® Baby Lash, Bulky (1¾ oz/50g), #67615 Soft 'n Sunny (cat toy)

Baby Bottle Covers: I used:
Ribbon
(instead of creating an I-cord if desired)
Black and white felt
MEDIUM 4
Needle and thread
(small bottle)
1 skein Red Heart® Super Saver™, Medium (7 oz/198g), #0672 Spring Green
(larger bottles—size of a water bottle also)
1 skein Red Heart® Super Saver™, Medium (7 oz/198g), #0324 Bright Yellow
1 skein Red Heart® Super Saver™, Medium (7 oz/198g), #0254 Pumpkin (for beak)
1 skein Red Heart® Super Saver™, Medium (7 oz/198g), #0885 Delft Blue

Baby Bottle Covers

This makes it easy for babies to hold onto their bottles especially when they are in the car. Your children can also create these to cover their water bottles, so they will instantly recognize theirs from all the others.

Instructions

1. Since yarn is medium weight, create lining and cover for each bottle. The smaller bottle requires a tube knitted lining 17 rows long, using two-over-two stitch on Knifty Knitter® Flower Loom. Larger bottle requires tube knitted lining 23 rows long, using two-over-two stitch on Flower Loom. Once linings are created, sew through loops on loom, remove, gather them together, and knot securely. Smaller bottle then requires tube knitted cover 19 rows long, using two-over-two stitch on Flower Loom. Larger bottle requires tube knitted cover 25 rows long, using two-over-two stitch on Flower Loom. Once covers are created, sew through loops on loom, remove and gather them together, and knot securely. Stuff lining inside cover piece.

2. To gather top around bottles, create I-cords or use ribbon. For bottles you need at least a 12" long I-cord or piece of ribbon, and sew this through top stitches of both lining and cover. Place cover on bottle and then tie two ends of I-cord or ribbon together with bow.

3. Using Knifty Knitter Pom-Pom & Tassel Maker create small pom-pom noses that you attach securely with thread or yarn strings—do not use glue. Create medium sized pom-poms for arms on each side. Cut out ovals in white felt or material, and smaller black material or felt circles to create eyes, and white felt or material for smiling mouths. Make sure you sew these on with needle and thread. For duck, I created pom-pom beak out of orange yarn, but I did not cut threads of pom-pom.

Note: Sewing everything on is preferred since you do not want a choking hazard and you will want to wash the bottle covers.

Candle or Bottle
Toppers

Baby Hat Candle Topper Instructions

Use as a baby shower gift or for any occasion.

1. Using white yarn, tube knit around entire Knifty Knitter® Flower Loom for 12 rows or 3". Fold bottom back on loom and knit to form band of hat.

2. Switch to blue yarn and knit for six more rows or 1½".

3. Sew through loops, remove from loom, and gather tightly. Knot and hide thread inside hat.

4. Make small white pom-pom on Pom-Pom & Tassel Maker. Add pom-pom to top of hat with white yarn.

5. Add hat to top of 5 oz. or 9 oz. candle of your choice.

Tree Candle Topper Instructions

This could also be placed over the top of a jar of candy.

1. Tube knit around entire Flower Loom until you have 1" of knitting. Fold bottom back on loom and knit to form band.
continued on page 92

Techniques
Tube knitting (see page 4)

Baby Hat Candle Topper
Materials Needed
Knifty Knitter® Flower Loom
Knifty Knitter Pom-Pom & Tassel Maker
1 skein white bulky yarn
1 skein blue bulky yarn
Yarn needle

BULKY 5

I used:
1 skein Bernat® Baby Lash, Bulky
(1¾ oz/50g), #67005 Wee White
1 skein Bernat® Baby Lash, Bulky
(1¾ oz/50g), #67143 Bunny Blue

Finished Size
3"–4" tall

Tree Candle Topper
Materials Needed
Knifty Knitter Flower Loom
1 skein green bulky yarn
White and red beads
Red ribbon and white ribbon
Yarn needle
Construction or heavyweight paper
Glue or glue gun
Clear adhesive tape

BULKY 5

I used:
1 skein Red Heart® Foxy™, Bulky
(1¾ oz/50g), #9630 Grass

Finished Size
4" tall

Candle or Bottle
Toppers continued

2. Continue knitting another 3" until you have total of 3½" including folded band.

3. Sew through loops, remove from loom, and gather together tightly. Turn inside out to furry side. Knot and hide thread inside tree.

4. Create funnel with construction or heavyweight paper. Glue or tape together to hold in place. Trim funnel to 3". Place inside knitted tree and place on lid of 5 oz. or 9 oz. candle.

5. Glue on beads like ornaments on tree. Tie two small red ribbon bows and slightly larger white bow. Glue red bow on each side of white bow and glue to top of tree.

Santa Hat Candle Topper Instructions

This could also be placed over a Mason jar filled with dry ingredients for a cookie recipe or homemade cocoa recipe.

1. Tube knit around entire Flower Loom using white yarn until you have 12 rows or 3". Fold bottom back on loom and knit to form band.

2. Switch to red yarn and knit 16 rows or 4".

Techniques
Tube knitting (see page 4)

Santa Hat Candle Topper Materials Needed
Knifty Knitter® Flower Loom
Knifty Knitter Pom-Pom & Tassel Maker
1 skein white bulky yarn
1 skein red bulky yarn
Yarn needle

BULKY 5

I used:
1 skein Bernat® Baby Lash, Bulky (1¾ oz/50g), #67005 Wee White
1 skein No Boundaries®, Bulky (50g/30 m), #24 Stella

Finished Size
About 8" long

3. Use yarn needle to sew through loops, remove from loom, and gather loops tightly together.

4. Make small white pom-pom on Pom-Pom & Tassel Maker. Add pom-pom to top of hat with white yarn.

5. Place hat on top of 26 oz. (or smaller) candle of your choice.

Chick blanket
page 22

Winter blanket
page 25

Baby's first quilt
page 28

Baby bear & blanket
page 31

Toddler sweater
page 35

Toy bag
page 38

Girl's shrug
page 42

Scarf & hat
page 44

Prairie scarf & hat
page 46

Afghan shawl
page 48

Mommy & me blanket
page 50

Baseball & basketball
pillows page 54

Broom horse
page 60

Pirate costume & boots
page 63

Fancy dress-up
page 66

Dice with family games
page 70

Journal book covers
page 76

Girls sleepover crafts
page 78

Bird marionette
page 80

Worm marionette
page 84

Have a ball crafts
page 86

Candle or bottle toppers
page 90